# Citadel of Sin:
# The John Looney Story

*Written by Richard Hamer and Roger Ruthhart*

*Best wishes*
*Roger Ruthhart*

**Published by**
Moline Dispatch Publishing Company, L.L.C.
1720 Fifth Avenue
Moline, IL 61265

Additional copies of this book can be ordered online at qconline.com/books.

ISBN: 978-0-9761162-8-8

# Citadel of Sin: The John Looney Story

## Contents

# Forward

The story of John Looney is worthy of some of the world's great fiction writers. The difference is that the story you are about to read is all true.

Years of reporting about Looney by the many newspapers that were the main source of news of the era form the foundation of this story. The authors thank the reporters of the Looney era for their diligence and generally factual reporting. The papers' detailed reports are supplemented by official police reports, trial transcripts, grand jury testimony and extensive interviews with people who were alive at the time, or whose relatives played key roles in the "Citadel of Sin" tale. The result is a fascinating look at the gangland world that was Rock Island in the early 20th century.

The story has been waiting to be told for decades. Many parts of it are community lore — shared and handed down from one generation to the next. Some parts have been previously committed to history through extensive newspaper reports.

There is one overriding reason why we have put the entire story together now, and why we dedicate this book to Max Allan Collins, Tom Hanks and Paul Newman. That reason is the movie "Road To Perdition." John Looney's lawless rein was the basis for the vivid story told in that popular movie, which was based on the graphic novel by Collins. Newman played a character called John Rooney, and there you begin to see the need for this historically accurate account. "Road To Perdition," while an impressive cinematic achievement, is not historically accurate. Not close. It didn't try to be. It's not even set in the correct decade and creates many false impressions for those who might rely on it for information about the real John Looney. If you want to set in your mind's eye the mood and attitudes of that dark and lawless era, then be sure to see the movie. If you are looking for facts about Looney's life and the people in it, you won't find them there.

To set the record straight, we offer this historical look at the life and times of John Looney. We hope you will agree that the real-life tale is better than fiction.

There are many stories about John Looney that have become part of the fabric of local lore. Only facts that we were convinced really happened, through corroboration by multiple sources, are part of this history about one of the nation's most powerful and ruthless gangland bosses. In some cases, we have offered several similar but differing accounts of important events. Talk to enough people, and you are sure to hear about friends or relatives who claimed to have done business with Looney. Most could not be independently substantiated. In fact, there are many stories we believe were concocted after the fact in an effort to become part of the Looney legend.

Common are stories about Al Capone and other gangsters visiting for parties, orgies and poker games with Looney. There is no evidence Capone ever set foot in Rock Island. During the Looney era, Capone was a lesser-known operative for Chicago's Johnny Torrio. Capone thought Looney was nuts and wanted nothing to do with him, and Capone's page in history was not to be written until a decade later. In reality, John Looney didn't have many business associates, and even fewer friends. There are many other great tales that have become part of local legend, which could not be independently verified. You won't find them in this book.

Also missing today are many of the Looney-era landmarks. Many have fallen to fire, the wrecking ball, or modern economic development. Some just fell into disrepair and almost collapsed. A few were eliminated by a city happy to embrace its historic past, but not this lurid portion of it. While most of the era's bars and brothels are gone, many of the historic homes of the time remain. Still standing as of this writing, are Looney's house, resembling a fortress on the hill, as well as Frank Kelly's elegant house across the street and another nearby Looney house known as "The Roost." All have been changed, remodeled and changed again over the years, but currently appear much as they did in the Looney era. Bel Air, Looney's home on the Rock River, has had the top floor removed and the remainder remodeled, so that it no longer resembles the great party mansion of the time. Development has sprung up all around it.

"Citadel of Sin: The John Looney Story" is a fascinating tale, with incredible twists and turns. It's a story of power and corruption; of sex, drugs and blackmail; of stolen cars, beautiful women, hooch, gun battles and murder. If we were starting out to write a book of pure fiction, we could not improve on Looney's real-life story.

This work represents more than a decade of research. It started innocently enough when local historian Richard Hamer was conducting historic trolley tours in Rock Island, pointing out the famous Looney landmarks. He began researching the gangster in order to provide a more complete commentary and to be able to answer the inevitable questions. The work snowballed from there. Roger Ruthhart, managing editor of The Rock Island Argus newspaper, began researching Looney for a series of stories published in conjunction with the newspaper's 150th anniversary in 2001. For more than two decades, the paper had been the archenemy of Looney and his Rock Island News.

Perhaps it was inevitable that the two writers should decide to collaborate on this effort — combining Rich's patience and research with Roger's writing skills. The result is a collaborative effort that will stand the test of history. It reveals many, many previously untold stories about one of the nation's most villainous criminals.

Rich would like to thank his many sources, friends and family, and especially his late wife, Jean, for their understanding and support through more than a decade of research. Roger would also like to thank his family and all of the journalists he has worked with through the years who helped keep the passion alive and made him a better writer. Both would like to thank the many, many sources that contributed to the book and the Moline Dispatch Publishing Co., L.L.C., and Small Newspaper Group, for helping this project become a reality.

# Home, home in Illinois

Railroad tracks slant gently along a curve of the Fox River and flow along a row of houses perched on the south ridge, then turn west past a scattering of houses and farms. A road leads past the Catholic cemetery on the crest of the hill, a sad journey for Irish families.

It was a hard road from County Kerry in Ireland, a country torn by hunger, English oppression and little hope. America would be better and spirits were high as many Irish streamed to America's shores. Millions of families fled in 1855 — among them Patrick and Margaret Looney. Patrick had been born in County Kerry, Ireland, in 1826 and Margaret in 1836. The family's name originally was O'Lowney, but the "O" was dropped and spelling changed along the way. Despite the changes, the name was still pronounced "Lowney" by some family members. Distance from their beloved Emerald Isle was required for survival, but it was never forgotten.

The church provided solace, but it didn't feed the family. Only hard work could do that. The parish priest was their conscience, but that didn't fill empty stomachs. You did what you must to eat. Early Irish in the United States were relegated to menial work as maids, miners, waiters, bartenders, dishwashers and ditch diggers. Politics became a natural magnet — it would change things and give them power. It was a way to gain a voice in America.

This was the world that John Looney grew up in as a boy.

*Mike Looney, John's uncle, owned a bar in Ottawa's Kerry Patch.*

*Mike and Patrick Looney, sons of John Looney's uncle, Mike.*

*This photo is an early one of John Looney, known to the family as Paddy John.*

South across the tracks was the heart of the city of Ottawa, Illinois, and just across the street from the Rock Island Lines depot was the modest home of Patrick and Margaret Looney, where John grew up. Later in life it was still the source of many memories; a place for John to come home to.

One such homecoming came just days after his father's death on Christmas Day in 1892. After a lingering illness, Patrick died at 3:30 Sunday afternoon at his home on Marquette Street at about age 65. Born in 1826, Patrick had spent much of his life in Ottawa after making the trip from Ireland via New York. His family was raised there and it was there that he would lie forever.

Patrick returned to St. Columba Church one last time for a 9:30 funeral on Tuesday and from there the procession of family and friends slowly left the tree-lined streets and climbed the hill to the wind-swept St. Columba Cemetery. The horses' hooves and wagon wheels stirred up only small puffs of dust as they moved along the frozen dirt roads. The cold winds whipped the faces of the dark-clad mourners, huddled together against death's bitter blasts.

With final prayers said, they all walked slowly back to the wagons that would return them to the hustle and bustle of life.

John lingered. He walked slowly, knowing he must return to the life he had been living in Rock Island since moving there in 1885. Paddy John, as the family called him, was flooded with memories of his family and childhood. Born in County Kerry, Ireland, his father had come to America as a young man in 1855. Like so many Irish families of the time, the trip was made a necessity by the potato famine at home. Patrick settled in New York, where his first daughter, Kate, was born. The family later made its way to Ottawa, where they settled in a heavily Irish area of town called the Kerry Patch after County Kerry.

Patrick Looney became a drayman for the Rock Island Lines, carrying goods to

*Kate Looney, left, John's older sister, and her cousins Hannah and Theresa.*

the local businesses. He was elected highway commissioner in 1887 and held that post until the spring before his death, when he retired because of poor health.

John's mind wandered as he remembered the days he worked with his father. He had learned how to tell a good horse from a bad one and how to train them. "Be firm, but never mean or angry. When giving commands, keep them simple," his father would tell him. Young John remembered watching his father with wide-eyed interest as he hitched the team. His father had a new lesson every day, whether with horses or life's other challenges. John listened carefully. He had an excellent teacher.

*John Looney's oldest sister, Kate*

He remembered with pride riding with his father on his rounds — a loaded wagon pulled south on Columbus Street toward downtown Ottawa. He remembered bursting with pride sitting next to the man he idolized and loved — doing a man's job. As a boy of 12, he was the envy of the Kerry Patch, as every evening after school he would help his father load his wagon at the Rock Island freight house, across the street from the family home, and make deliveries around town.

John never had time to play games with the other boys, a friend later recalled. "He wasn't inept. He was coordinated, competitive and strong for a youngster," his friend said. He also hated to lose at anything. "If angered he would fly into a rage and both fists would swing no matter how big the opponent. When John was beaten until he couldn't stand up, he would tell them, 'I'll get you next time. Ya can't whip me,' " his friend said.

As the winter wind almost blew his hat away, John remembered his father arriving home late each night, hungry and tired. His mother and sister, Kate, would fix the meal while Patrick cleaned up.

As he walked out of the cemetery and got close to the wagons, John recalled with fondness the family gatherings in the parlor on Sunday after the meal. His father would tell stories about life in Ireland. Tears would flow down his face as he described the magnificent beauty of the country. Many times he would tell his favorite story about the Irish patriot, Robert Emmet, who fought and died seeking Irish independence. He would rise up from his chair, arms stretched above his head, fists clenched in defiance and racked with emotion as he told how Emmet was captured and executed. Emmet was partially hung, disemboweled and beheaded before the citizens of Dublin.

When he was finished, Patrick Looney would fall back into his chair exhausted, his family silent and speechless.

*Norah Looney, wife of Mike Looney, who was John's uncle and ran a bar in Ottawa.*

"Let them and me repose in obscurity and peace, and my tomb remain uninscribed, until other times, and other men, can do justice to my character; when my country takes her place among the nations of the earth, then and not till then let my epitaph be written," Emmet had said. Patrick Looney would utter Emmet's last words again and again. His fate and spirit would affect John Looney throughout his life.

John climbed in the wagon and started back down the hill toward town. The slow clomps of the horses provided a relaxing rhythm and a slower pace to his life, even if for just a few moments while the winter wind pulled at his hat. As the funeral procession arrived at the family home and food started appearing from all directions, John remembered how special Sunday dinner had been when he was growing up. His sister, Kate, would go to early Mass and be home preparing dinner before the rest of the family returned from church. Baked chicken or roast lamb, with baked bread and pie, was the usual Sunday fare. And always mounds of potatoes — a custom that drove them from the old country. Lack of potatoes meant hunger, John reflected sentimentally. He could recall those warm and tempting smells as if it were yesterday.

Later in life, John told friends that the nuns didn't really like him because he frequently forgot the church rules. He thought about those services as he walked into the house. His trademark smirk was visible, as it had been even as a young boy.

John was often overconfident and ambitious to a fault. He would give his father advice on how to make deliveries faster and more efficiently, and Patrick would listen with interest and then tell his son not to take short cuts in life. "It's hard work it is that makes you a living. You work twice as hard as the other fellows and always keep your word. That's most important. And finish what you started, right or wrong," Patrick Looney would tell his son.

As he waited for the guests to leave, John's mind wandered. He recalled sneaking out of the same house on Saturday nights and running down the alley to his Uncle Mike's bar. There he would take up a spot at the end of the bar and watch the drunks and gamblers — most of them neighbors and friends. The Germans, who lived on the other side of the Kerry Patch, would come in and buy beer by the buckets to take home and drink. At the bar, John learned to play poker at an early age, and he learned that the Irish will bet on just about anything.

His Uncle Mike knew he was there, but didn't seem to care. When things got out of hand, Mike would push the brawlers out the door. Mike wasn't above getting in trouble with the law himself from time to time. John didn't like the drinking and smoking — and vowed he would never do either. But he was always delighted when there was combat. Looney's mother once said, "Paddy John isn't happy unless there's turmoil. Trouble seems to find him wherever he goes."

Her words would prove prophetic.

As the funeral reception quieted down, John looked around the house at the gathered family. John was the oldest boy among eight children. His oldest sister, Kate, was eight years older and Margaret, or Maggie, was two years older, being the first of the Looney family born in Ottawa in 1864. After John, born November 5, 1866, came Jeremiah or Jerry, Timothy and William — each spaced two years apart. The baby, Edward, was nine years younger than John, born in 1875. Jerry, like John, would go to Rock Island, where he became a train dispatcher. Will would escape charges of embezzlement while working at the Ottawa Fair Dealer newspaper and spend a short time in the newspaper business with his brother in Rock Island before moving to Indiana.

*John and Nora Looney's residence, located at the corner of Marquette and Paul streets in Ottawa, as it appeared in more modern times.*

John sadly remembered returning home just one year earlier for the death of his sister, Anna. She had developed lung trouble in January of that year and, after being treated in Ottawa and Chicago, it was decided that a change in climate was needed. She left for Texas, but her improvement was only temporary and she died in September at age 22. She was considered bright, amiable and well-cultured. Her loss was a tragic one to the family, especially happening so far away, although her mother had traveled to San Antonio to be with her. Hundreds of friends visited the Looney home after her death, and her funeral cortege was reported to be one of the longest the city had ever seen.

She was buried in an unmarked grave at St. Columba Cemetery.

There were other Looneys who lived in Ottawa, too. While some relatives would leave to go west, and others to Chicago, many would remain in LaSalle

County, where their descendents still live today. And in the Irish community, even those who weren't family sometimes seemed as if they were.

While John's father was urging him to work hard each day for a hard-earned wage, his mother was pushing John and the others to have a better life. Her dream for the children was a life better than she was able to give them. John would use her encouragement as justification for cutting corners and cheating. As a result, he hated to lose at anything and would do anything to get ahead. The philosophy would get him in trouble later in life.

His mother's brother, uncle Maurice T. Moloney, was a powerful local figure and politician who also pushed the children to get ahead. The success of the former state Attorney General, city attorney and mayor of Ottawa, and LaSalle County state's attorney, pushed John toward a career in law and later an attempt at elected office. Moloney used his power and connections to get John a job as a telegrapher for Western Union at the Rock Island train station in Ottawa. He started there in 1881 at age 15.

John's younger brother, Jeremiah, also benefited from his uncle's connections. He received business training from P.L. Cable of the Rock Island Railroad and then went west to Colorado, where in 1894 he was appointed receiver of the United States Land Office in Sterling, Colorado.

John's sister, Margaret, and a neighbor, Nora O'Connor, started a millinery business and traveled to New York and Europe to bring the latest fashions back to Ottawa. The die was likely cast for John's future when in July 1890, his mother and Miss O'Connor cemented their friendship while taking a three-month cruise to Ireland. It wasn't long before John found himself pushed into the company of Nora O'Connor by his mother.

On September 28, 1892, Margaret married Michael Pendergast of the powerful Pendergast political family. With Mrs. Looney pulling the strings, it was perhaps less of a coincidence than many thought when the wedding turned into a double wedding with John and Nora, scheduled to be a bridesmaid and groomsman, also being married on the same day. By then, John had passed the bar and opened his law practice in Rock Island.

John remembered the day when he and Nora surprised the assembled relatives and close friends with the double wedding in the front parlor of this very house. Maggie and Michael stood before a bank of shamrocks and marguerites in the northeast corner of the parlor. After the couple completed their vows, they exchanged places with John, 27, and Nora, 26, and the Rev. Dean Thomas Keating went through the ceremonies once again — to the pleasant surprise of everyone present. A joint bridal dinner followed and then a reception until 4 o'clock, when the Pendergasts left for their Michigan honeymoon. Nora remained in Ottawa to run her millinery emporium, while John returned to his law practice in Rock Island. There was little doubt that Mrs. Looney was behind both Margaret's millinery partnership and John's wedding to Nora O'Connor.

As John lay down that night and closed his eyes, childhood memories flashed through his head. He remembered all of the things he had done with his father. He remembered the stories about the breath-taking beauty of Ireland, the happy and sad moments from the day's gathering of family and friends, and the storied history of Emmet. He smiled slightly and sighed as he thought of his father's unmarked grave — not far from that of his sister. That was the way it should be.

# A mighty good line

*Early photo of John Looney*

For towns that had one, the railroad station was a center of the community in the late 1800s. It was the link to the outside world, a place where business was conducted and where personal and business travel became intertwined. Ottawa was no different, and John Looney grew up across the street from the Rock Island Lines depot there.

The station in Ottawa was busy, welcoming freight and passengers as they moved from Chicago to Rock Island and points west. Besides passenger and freight facilities, it had a corn crib, coal shed, a water tank, locomotive feeder and express office, as well as a flag house for the crossing at Columbus Street. Trains would pass through in both directions many times a day. Smoke, cinders, and the echoing howl of the steam whistles were part of daily life for the Looneys and others who lived in the Kerry Patch.

When John Looney was 15, he learned telegraphy at the Western Union Company office located at the depot. In November 1885, Looney, now 18 and night operator for three years, was promoted and put in charge of the city telegraph station at Rock Island. He began his duties there November 23.

The move would change his life forever.

Rock Island in the late 19th century was a bustling commercial center where railroads and the rivers met and became forever linked. To Rock Island's south, John found picturesque bluffs stretching to the sheltered valley of the Rock River and scenery of unrivaled beauty. Comfortable residences dotted the sides of these hills, amid clumps of trees and miniature forests that afforded shelter and shade to the wealthy. The famous water power produced by the upper Mississippi rapids contributed to the marvelous growth of this city.

In Rock Island, John Looney found a flourishing town with factories manufacturing plows, cultivators and other agricultural appliances, as well as wagons and carriages. There were foundries and machine shops to support the efforts. At night, the streets were lit with electric lights and the sidewalks paved and clean. Rock Island had a well-organized police force, a fire department, waterworks, street cars, a flourishing public library, free postal delivery, churches and public schools. Five railroads passed through the city, making it the center of railroading in the region. It had one of the few railroad bridges across the Mississippi River, and its commerce and trade were second to no city of its size.

Train engines belched smoke and steam whistles happily announced trains' arrival and departure. There was a general bustle around town that gave it a feel of being a vibrant and active place. John saw it as a city of opportunity.

He noticed that the residences all had neat yards and he dreamed of some day owning his own house on the bluff. The shrubbery and flowers clustered around the doorways of even the humblest residences offered a clear sign of comfortable living for the residents. This was the almost idyllic city John Looney found when he took his new job at age 18. It was growing with business opportunities, but the Tri-Cities of Rock Island, Moline and Davenport also were developing some of the rowdiness and lawlessness that John Looney later would learn to thrive on.

For some time, John lived a double life, and that's the way he wanted it. He had one foot squarely planted in Rock Island and the other still in Ottawa. He took a sleeping room during the week and then took the train home to be with his family on the weekends. He was immature, but studious and ambitious, and his desire to succeed and get ahead soon became an all-consuming passion. As time passed, John Looney became more and more integrated into the life of Rock Island.

John was anxious to rise above his post in the telegraph office. By age 21, he decided that the study of law offered his quickest route to prominence, and with the urging of prominent attorneys John Kenworthy and Adair Pleasants, he borrowed law books and studied at night while working in the Western Union office during the day. John had always loved to read, and he was drawn to newspapers and cheap novels like a moth to a lamp. From them he drew a fascination with the West. The exploits of Billy the Kid and the James Gang were played out in the newspaper headlines of his day, further feeding his fascination with the Wild West. John also joined a literary club, named after prominent contractor and builder Matthias Schnell. With Schnell promoting him, he began to climb the social and political ladder. John Looney's confidence and arrogance climbed along with him.

By 1889, John Looney, not yet 23, was president of the Fifth Ward Democratic Club and controlled several city precincts. After much hard work, he passed the state bar examination in Illinois and became a law partner with Frank H. Kelly. Kelly had been born in Rock Island in 1870 and educated at the University of Michigan after attending Rock Island schools. At five feet eight inches, 125 pounds, John Looney was not an imposing figure, but he grew in stature nonetheless. His star was continuing to rise.

When John left his job with Western Union in December 1890, his younger brother replaced him. Tim also had taken his previous job in Ottawa. Tim Looney returned to Ottawa to marry Catharine Marie Casey on October 22, 1891. She was the daughter of retired farmer William Casey, and the reception was at her parents' home in Grand Ridge. The couple moved to Denver, Colorado, in December.

On January 20, 1891, the circuit court in Rock Island heard the case of Frank Wilson, who was charged with residential burglary. It was John's first case since beginning active practice. The local newspaper, The Rock Island Argus, reported that he "made an able effort in behalf of his client." The jury found Wilson guilty and sentenced him to one year in the penitentiary. John was disappointed, but not discouraged. The next day, he tried a forgery case and lost it, too. They would be the first of many criminals that John Looney would defend.

Beyond his law office, John was determined to grow and extend his personal contacts.

He wrote, produced and directed the play "Emmet" about the Irish rebel that had meant so much to his family and others living in the Kerry Patch. He played the part of Emmet and was proud and excited when it was presented just days after his first court case. As he wrote the lines for the part, and then prepared to take the stage, he could see and hear his father in his mind's eye — expressing the passion and love for Emmet as he told and retold the stories of his patriotism. Having grown up with Emmet, it was easy, it seemed, for John to transform his father's passion to the stage. He earned great reviews from The Argus, which called his speech at the end of the play magnificent. The play was staged at the Harper Opera House on January 23, 1891.

His many return trips to Ottawa resulted in the September 28, 1892, surprise marriage to Nora O'Connor. A 21st century career couple more than a century ahead of their time, she would stay in Ottawa to run her millinery store while John continued to commute and build his law practice. In November 1892, John and Nora bought a home in Ottawa at the corner of Marquette and Paul streets, next to his parents' home at 117 Marquette Street.

John Looney's law practice was growing. He was a good-hearted man, always ready to help the poor and never making a great deal of money from his practice. Often he found those he was helping were Irish immigrants. Many times he lost hopeless cases while receiving little, if any, pay for his efforts. He fought many cases in which he knew the client could never pay his fee and would give legal advice for free to those who were less fortunate.

While defending low-life criminals accused of petty crimes against residents of Rock Island, he became acquainted with hundreds of characters from the underworld. More often than not, he would lose, but his practice gave him insight and connections within the underworld that eventually would become a way of life. He learned court procedures and how to manipulate the law for his benefit. He was building the beginning of his empire while making money and developing acquaintances on a higher social level. One of those was Matthias Schnell.

Schnell was German-born and immigrated to this country. He married an Irish bride in New York City and eventually settled in Rock Island, where he was in business for more than 50 years. He built more than 100 hospitals and churches across the country and was also awarded the contract for the state capitol building in Austin, Texas. He developed a large tract of land in south Rock Island for new homes, and many prominent businessmen, including the famed architect George P. Stauduhar and builder Nicolai E. Juhl, started their careers with him.

Schnell was a leader of the community, serving as alderman, a promoter of literary events, a political power and contributor to many charities. He befriended young John Looney, fell under Looney's spell and promoted him as one of the most brilliant young men of the Tri-Cities. Without his support, John could not have gained the recognition he needed to fulfill his lofty dreams and ambitions.

The dark clouds that would shroud much of his life began gathering in September 1897, when John Looney and his law partner, Frank Kelly, along with Schnell and others they were defending, were implicated in a scandal over construction of the 24th Street storm drain. They were indicted for defrauding the city by using inferior materials. John Looney had finally come to the fork in the road that divided good and evil, and he took the first steps in a long journey down the wrong road.

Schnell had backed the sewer line project at Looney's request. The sewers were built of brick and Looney secretly had the contractor switch bags of cement, exchanging high-quality material for an inferior, cheaper product. The contract also called for concrete for backfill around and under the drains, but common dirt, sand and loose stones were used. The switch was discovered and The Argus ripped Schnell and Looney as co-conspirators. Looney was fined the maximum $2,000 and his partner, Frank Kelly, was issued a $1,500 fine. Four others were fined amounts ranging from $200 down to $1. Schnell never recovered from the publicity and fell in disrepute as a builder. Looney crime lieutenant Dan Drost later would claim that his boss robbed his benefactor of more than $50,000 — quite a sum in that day.

Looney fought the court action for more than a decade. There were convictions, but they were overturned on appeal in April 1899, and the case never was retried. Schnell ended his career despondent in a rented apartment, while the incident, more than any other, marked the beginning of Looney's turn to the dark side. He saw new ways in which power could be used to his advantage, and his hunger for control never subsided from that point forward.

Almost simultaneously with Looney's indictment, in his other world in Ottawa, Nora Looney opened O'Connor's Millinery Store on October 1, 1897, after ending her partnership with John's sister, Mrs. Pendergast.

"Mrs. Looney will put before the public the largest and grandest stock of millinery ever

*An early photo of Kathleen Looney, John and Nora's oldest daughter, who would take the vows of a nun and leave the area after graduation from Villa de Chantal.*

shown in LaSalle County. In fact, the store will be the most complete west of Chicago," the local newspaper reported.

With a place of their own to call home, it was not long before John and Nora began a family. Their first daughter, Kathleen, was born July 14, 1894, followed by Ursula Mary on December 2, 1898. Both were born in Ottawa. A son, John Connor, would be born later, November 19, 1900, after Nora and the family finally had joined John in Rock Island.

In 1900, John Looney appeared in the headlines once again after deciding to run for the Illinois Legislature. But John wasn't part of the area's power elite, and to some he was not to be trusted. The Argus became aware of Looney's dishonorable plan to divide the Democratic Party's election of delegates to the Presidential Convention by rigging votes for himself. The Argus reminded the public of this plan every day, and not only was Looney defeated in his bid for public office, he was disgraced. He also learned a powerful and lasting lesson about the power of the press.

John was driven to get even. In 1905 he started his own newspaper, The Rock Island News. John managed the paper along with his two brothers, Will, a reporter, and Jerry, the typesetter.

"As most lawyers are, I was forced into politics," John said later. "I happened to get under the shadow of the ill will of what we call the money element in Rock Island, Illinois, very early in my political career."

Looney's relationship with The Argus would continue to be stormy.

"On every possible occasion The Argus would write me up, and on several occasions when I carried conventions it would put in belting conversations against me and create disturbances which always, however, ended in a tribute to me," John Looney said, telling the story from his side.

"They kept this up for years. I started the Daily Rock Island News to try to offset these attacks, and the effort was successful. From the day I started, they ceased even mentioning my name in The Argus," John related, inaccurately, years later. "I exposed them and their clique."

The cities of that era were ripe for lawlessness and John Looney wasn't the only man profiting from it. By the turn of the century, the towns were hoppin' and most of it wasn't legal. An old-time saloon keeper recalled the era saying, "I'll tell you about a town so tough it made Chicago look like an old-people's home."

It all started in Davenport, Iowa, before the turn of the century.

"They called it Bucktown — six blocks of complete, unadulterated sin, right at the foot of the Arsenal's Government Bridge," the saloonkeeper recalled. "The New York Tribune said it was the 'worst town in America, bar none. New York is a milk town compared to Davenport.' There's Perl Galvin's bar known as the ultimate of sin. Naughty girls hung umbrellas and panties over the back bar of old Perly's place. If you got out of there still a virgin, it was a miracle.

"There were over 200 saloons in Davenport and most were located in Bucktown, running wide open 24 hours a day, 7 days a week. Some of them dumps didn't own keys for the doors. Most of them had wine rooms in the rear of the saloon for con men, thieves and whores to make deals with the suckers."

Painted ladies freely roamed the streets and gambling houses and whorehouses were open and without restraint. A bunch called the John C. Mabray Gang, known all over the country as tough con men, made its headquarters in Bucktown — taking dummies for millions.

*Brick Munro*

"Along with the saloons and sporting houses were sleazy theaters, real low-life burlesque acts, women whispering in men's ears making propositions to them, and lewd acts were held at some of the back-alley places," the old-timer remembered. "The Bijou, The Standards, The Orpheum and the biggest was The Pavilion, owned by the King of Bucktown, Brick Munro. He would entertain a thousand people on a single night. He had a gold mine.

"Davenport's gambling houses were famous all over the nation. The Eldorado, The Senator, The Saratoga and The Ozark had poker games running three or four days a week. Bert Smith was the bookmaker who promoted most of the games. He hung out at The Hot Springs, a wild place. Slot machines were everywhere — cigar stores, pool halls, dance halls, whorehouses, and I saw some in bathrooms," the barkeep continued.

Bucktown roared with ragtime pianos and sporting houses flourished. Big Cal Harris, with his checkered vest, promoted illegal fist fights in warehouses. Bare knuckle, anything-goes tough guys floated from town to town playing the crowd, and they loved Bucktown. You could bet on anything that moved — dog fights, cock fights, arm wrestling. Ringers would be imported from St. Louis or New Orleans.

"Negro musicians drifted north from Memphis, or Kansas City, and worked the whore houses — sometimes working for room, board, whores and booze. Al Jolson, on his way west in his younger days, was drawn to the place as a singing waiter. He sang for tips and beer. He never forgot Davenport, especially Brick Munro's place," the saloonkeeper said.

Bucktown howled into the 20th century with a snootful of booze and law enforcement in its hip pocket. However, as bad as Davenport was, Rock Island was just as bad. One reformer said, "If Davenport is hell, Rock Island is the chimney." When Bucktown finally hit the skids, Rock Island stepped up and took its place.

John Looney was there to lead the way, and in time would reign over a crime empire that not only encompassed Rock Island and Davenport, but spread up and down the river from Missouri to Wisconsin and had tentacles that spanned the country. Locals tended to see him as being involved in local corruption, but his power reached far beyond that.

John lived two different lives — some would say with different personalities — in Rock Island and Ottawa. But in 1899, Nora, pregnant with her third child, finally insisted that the family live together.

Early in his career, John and his partner Frank Kelly went into real estate development in a big way, developing an addition east of 20th Street and south of 16th Avenue to be known as the Highland Park addition of Rock Island. John Looney bought a lot from Kelly and his wife, Anna, for one dollar. In 1897, he built a 6,000-square-foot home at 1635 20th Street — across the street from the Kellys. The Looney house started out as a reproduction of the Kellys' graceful Queen Anne, which was designed by architect George Stauduhar. At first, Looney's plans were identical, but then his house had to be bigger and better. He added porches

*John Looney's main home, at 1635 20th Street, today remains relatively unchanged on the exterior.*

*John Looney had a second home, known as "The Roost" at 2012 16th Avenue. It was located near his main house and was where his henchmen gathered and where his newspaper was printed at one time.*

on three levels, stone pedestals, and brick and stone veneer on the exterior instead of wood, giving it a fortress-like appearance. All of the interior rooms where people congregated were luxurious. The first level had inlaid floors in rosewood, ebony, walnut and oak. The library built-ins were of sycamore and the dining room built-ins were of oak. The original house also featured several stained-glass and beveled-glass windows, five fireplaces and a wide, rounded oak staircase.

In August 1899, Looney bought another lot from the Kellys in his wife's name. This lot would eventually be home to "The Roost," located at 2012 16th Avenue, where he published his paper for a time.

A few short years later, on May 4, 1903, Nora died of cancer after an extended illness and several operations on her spine in Chicago. By then, her husband had already had his first run-in with the law. John was left to raise the children by himself, and by most accounts didn't do a very good job.

Nora was remembered later by a friend as an attractive and gentle lady with a ready smile and a pleasing disposition. She was small of build with pale skin and very delicate looking but was a fierce worker who did everything that needed to be done at her business in Ottawa. She greeted shoppers with her friendly Irish accent and made most of the sales in her store. She was liked by all who knew her, belonged to many local organizations and spent many hours collecting money for charitable causes as well as spending time with her family and church.

*John Looney's home on the Rock River, known as Bel Air, was removed from the rest of the city in those days. It was known for some of the underworld's greatest parties, gambling and drunken orgies. It still stands, but has been significantly remodeled.*

*Looney's Bel Air hideout also had a large barn that provided a club and athletic rooms, as well as room to store carriages and cars.*

In August 1903, John purchased another lot in the addition from his brother-in-law, James O'Connor and his wife, Kittie, and the Kellys. It was also after Nora's death that he purchased 37 acres of land on the Rock River in February of 1904. Here he built his second home, Bel Air, and a large two-story barn with a high basement. The barn was begun that summer and built near the head of a hollow, completely surrounded by hills and trees so that even the roof was scarcely visible. It was built of dark-colored stone 18 inches thick. The basement was high enough that carriages could be driven inside and the upper two floors were devoted to a club and athletic rooms for Looney's guests.

The three-story house was built the next year as a safe haven and getaway for his gang of thugs. The land was heavily wooded with a long drive out to a country lane called Black Hawk Road. The house was built of limestone block from a quarry in nearby Milan.

Bel Air was removed from the rest of the world, with no neighbors near by and plenty of opportunity to see if someone was approaching. It would become the heart of Looney's criminal empire, and its third-floor ballroom would host some of the underworld's greatest parties, gambling and drunken orgies. In 1914, Looney would add a 20,000-acre ranch in New Mexico to his holdings.

## A Night Thought

The night stole softly up the sky,
  The song-birds sank to sleep,
And from the darkening heaven above
  The stars began to peep.

A hush fell o'er all living things,
  The queen of night held sway;
She waved her wand and lo! the world
  Forgot the weary day.

—KATHLEEN LOONEY.

Looney daughters Kathleen, or Kay, and Ursula were enrolled at the Villa de Chantel — a Catholic girls' boarding school near their main home in Rock Island. In her junior year, Kathleen was elected class president and was so efficient in the office that she was re-elected her senior year and was also business manager of the yearbook staff. Kathleen would take her vows to become a Catholic nun at The Villa, the Monastery of The Sisters of the Visitation in Rock Island, and later move to a convent in St. Louis. Looney lieutenant Dan Drost later claimed that he paid for Kathleen to leave for the convent to help her get away from Looney. Drost said Looney never forgave him for it.

Ursula was not able to escape her father until she married Frank Hamblin and even then only at an arm's length. Drost said that Looney forced her to write scandal news for his newspaper and be involved in things that a young girl shouldn't even know about.

"In front of witnesses she said, 'My father would sell me, body and soul, for money.' His own daughter," said Drost.

"All Looney's daughters got away from him. All his daughters shrank from him and despised him. They all knew he was crooked and a criminal — they saw he was laying out a crooked path for them," said Drost.

Looney's son, Connor, never escaped the black cloud that followed his father. With the girls at The Villa, Connor and his father lived in filth in the house on the hill. Connor's involvement in his father's gang eventually would lead to his untimely death. Drost said that Connor didn't approve of what his father did either.

"Not a member of Black Jack's family will have anything to do with him. All of them hate and loathe him. He started out in life years ago by cheating his old mother out of all she had and left her penniless. He cheated his own sister, and all his brothers he has 'done' at different times," said Drost, including brother Bill, who later changed his name.

Long-time Rock Island resident Lewis B. Wilson attended Lincoln School with Connor and college with Ursula. He later characterized young Connor as "a nice kid when I knew him. The kids envied him — he came to school on a pony. As I remember him later, he was about five feet, eight inches tall, quiet and well-mannered." Ursula, he said, was moderately good looking, quiet, slender and about five feet, five inches tall.

*Ursula Looney*

Another friend of Ursula's, Miss Marguerite Reidy, said, "She resembled her father, with dark hair, high cheek bones, a good dresser and very personable. She wasn't allowed to stay at The Roost, because Dan Drost was there and he considered him a low-life character. I remember The Roost as very creepy, one light bulb hung over an oak table — nothing much else was in the room.

"Ursula had a gun under her pillow because her father said she should keep it there for protection. She fought for her father constantly and was very defiant if anything was said about him. When he went to jail, Ursula told me she would leave Rock Island and never come back — never. 'I will severe all connections with this area. No one will ever find us,' she said. She wasn't heard from again, as far as I know," said Miss Reidy.

The farm, on a bluff south of town overlooking the Rock River, was designed to serve as a citadel of sin — removed from the eyes of the community. Drost said that Looney starved his animals and was mean to his tenants.

"No man or animal ever dealt with him without regretting it," said Drost. "Looney was a cheap cock-fighter and dog-fighter. This shows his humanity and Christian charity." He would tie up dogs and go away and forget where he put them, only to find them dead later. Likewise, he would drop game chickens into a barrel and forget them, later finding them dead.

"This devilish thing went on for years at what he called the farm, now known as Prostitute Park," Drost said in 1922.

John was heartbroken by Nora Looney's death, but she never lived to see her husband become one of the nation's most powerful vice lords. Like his father and sister, John Looney buried Nora in an unmarked grave — in Rock Island's Chippiannock Cemetery.

# Extra! Extra!

John Looney saw the power that the Rock Island Argus newspaper wielded in the community and decided it was power he must have if he was going to get ahead in Rock Island. He blamed The Argus for crushing his political career, and he wanted to get even.

In 1905, Looney bought a building at 1817 Second Avenue, in the heart of downtown. In its original configuration it housed Looney's law offices on the second floor, the Mirror Lounge on the first floor, and the newspaper offices in a room behind the lounge. The Mirror Lounge had the finest food in town and was the most luxurious club in the Tri-Cities. The floors were inlaid marble and it had expensive mahogany paneling and the back bar was ornately carved wood. There were dazzling light fixtures and mirrors on the sidewalls and the ceiling. Out back, a stairway led upstairs to women who would sell sexual favors.

Looney's brother, William (Bill), followed in his brother's footsteps and in 1891 became an agent for the Western Pacific Railroad in Madison, Colorado. He returned to run the Ottawa Fair Trader newspaper until December 1897, when he resigned after being charged with embezzlement — of which he was found innocent. John brought Bill, and younger brother Jeremiah or Jerry, to Rock Island to run The News. The paper made little pretense of printing real news. Most of the articles attacked The Argus, but others claimed to expose citizens with deep dark secrets by writing exaggerated stories about them, which were beyond belief. For a fee, victims could have the story killed. "Kill Fees" varied by the victim's ability to pay. By the early 1900s, Looney was regularly lining his pockets with blackmail money.

*W. William Wilmerton*

Looney, of course, claimed otherwise.

"I took up the fight for the people, the poor, then the underdog and the taxpayer. I showed in my paper, for instance, that presidents of banks in Rock Island in filing schedules of property had perjured themselves and I charged these bank presidents with perjury in connection with these tax evasions.

"I went further than this. I showed where the editor of The Argus did not pay one cent of taxes. I kept up that sort of fight for years. I showed where corporations

*Crowds gathered outside the Rock Island News offices on Second Avenue one morning in late 1908 after dynamite was used to destroy the paper's press. It happened the day after John Looney lost an effort to swindle W. William Wilmerton in a stock sale. Looney was the prime suspect but was never charged.*

were doing the same thing, dodging their taxes. I found that the more money people had, the more they wanted to keep untaxed. Occasionally I was hired to defend persons under arrest, but my chief work was to show up the gambler, the pick-pockets and the officials who were busy robbing the public treasury," Looney bragged. In reality he was the worst of them all. He had many enemies in town as a result, but his power was growing.

Looney's spending habits were well known, and by 1908 Looney needed money to keep his many enterprises running. W. William Wilmerton, a wealthy but naïve farmer from rural Preemption who was unsuspecting of Looney's business tactics, agreed to buy controlling interest in The News. Looney never intended to give up control; he just wanted to obtain money to cover his debts elsewhere. But Wilmerton turned the tables on Looney. Looney was outraged.

About 2:30 a.m. the night after Wilmerton took over the newspaper, a dynamite bomb shattered the press in the building at 1817 Second Avenue. Publication was suspended.

The explosion extensively damaged the west side of the building, which housed the newspaper offices, but there was also damage to the east. The pressroom was on the extreme back, near the alley.

"The dynamite or other high explosive which was used was apparently placed on the press and attached to a fuse extending to the corridor door," The Argus reported. "The press is practically a complete wreck, and the entire interior

*This photo from the era looks west on Third Avenue between 18th and 19th streets, where the Looney-Wilmerton gun battle took place. The Fort Theater, now Circa '21 Dinner Playhouse, stands on the front left corner today.*

of the publication rooms, with the exception of the composing room, was wrecked."

Myron Jordan, acting editor of The News, who lived on the third floor, said a deal had been completed the previous night where Wilmerton secured stock of the company.

"Yesterday the actual payment of cash was made and the new owners held a meeting. Plans were begun to move the newspaper from the Looney building. Neither John nor W.C. (Bill) Looney was to have any further connection with the publication and would not have been here today had it not been for this explosion," Jordan said. He hinted that John Looney was responsible for the blast.

Wilmerton confirmed that the Looney brothers would have no involvement in The News. "I bought the whole business and will run it without them," he said.

Looney owned the building, which had been the target of a long, drawn-out mortgage foreclosure fight with G.A. Koester of Davenport, who had been a Looney benefactor. Two days after the explosion, The Argus reported that it would be difficult to convince people the Looneys were not still involved in The News.

"It may be necessary to go even further, even to the obliteration of the name, which has come to represent in the eyes of the decent people of this community all the odious practices to which any element of the public press may be degraded," The Argus said.

As a result of the blast, Looney was unable to create scandal via newsprint for almost a year. Under Wilmerton, The News became The Tri-City Morning Journal. Looney resumed publication of The News on February 6, 1909, this time from a garage on the side of the hill at his home known as "The Roost" at 2012 16th Avenue. Later, in 1924, he would move his printing press to the upper story of his mansion on the Rock River.

"Wilmerton broke his contract, so I took it back," said Looney of his paper.

Two mysterious blazes followed the dynamite attack and the removal of The News from the Looney building. The first, on November 2, 1908, ruined the Mirror Saloon, operated by Looney associate Dan Drost. When Looney refused a $7,000 insurance settlement, the company canceled his policy. On November 23, the day before the cancellation took effect — and just as a suit for collection of $32,000 indebtedness against the building was to be filed — a second fire did another $75,000 in damage to the building.

Drost later confirmed that Looney started the fire after first burglarizing the courthouse.

"Looney was behind in his mortgage payments to Koester and wanted to steal or fix the records in his favor. After he stole the records at the courthouse, he climbed over the transom and came out with a book, which he carried under his coat. He walked past the Woodmen Building and took the book to his home where he lived on the hill. He wore a fake beard," said Drost.

"Witnesses didn't know it was Looney running out of his building shouting FIRE! Looney came out disguised as a coal hauler, dressed in a chinchilla coal hauler's jacket with the collar turned up, a red bandana around his head, slouch hat pulled over his foretop," Drost said. Drost later admitted that he helped him burn the building.

Bill Looney left town soon after, and Drost said it was because he was ashamed that his brother had burned the building. He moved to Indiana and changed his name to Lowney because he couldn't stand his brother's crooked stunts and did not want to be associated with him. "He did not let Black Jack know where he moved because Black Jack would follow him and blackmail him," Drost said.

Looney couldn't forget the damage done to his publishing empire as a result of the battles with Wilmerton. It consumed him — even as he regained control of The News and began printing it again. In a sense, Looney was powerless without his newspaper, and he blamed Wilmerton, even though his own crooked scheme was the real cause. When Looney renewed publication of The News, he couldn't wait to attack Wilmerton in the first issue. This brought a reply from Wilmerton. But Looney had rolled up his sleeves and dug himself in. In the next issue of his paper, he wrote a scathing and bitter personal attack on Wilmerton and his family. The two really came to blows on February 22, 1909, in a downtown shootout that was like something out of a Hollywood movie.

"The expected happened this afternoon at 4:20 when W.W. Wilmerton and John Looney met near Nineteenth Street on Third Avenue and indulged in an affray with pistols," The Argus reported. "Both proved poor shots, Looney being hit in the side … Both were placed under arrest."

The gunfight occurred as the business day was winding down. Looney was heading from his office to a meeting with another attorney in the Safety Building at the southeast corner of Third Avenue and Eighteenth Street. It was a brisk winter day, and Looney took a shortcut from his office on Second Avenue down an alley running between Second and Third Avenues. Wilmerton was standing in the vestibule in front of the Morning Journal's office, just east of the Safety Building, when he saw Looney on the opposite side of the street.

He walked to his desk, threw up the roll top, slid it down again and walked to the door. By this time Looney was on the north side of the street about midway between the curb and the street car track. The two were 20 to 25 feet apart when Looney reached into his coat pocket and pulled out his revolver. He aimed and fired.

Pop — the shot rang out. Pop — another.

Wilmerton walked across the sidewalk, aimed and fired. Bang.

Both men retreated to the sidewalk, guns blazing, to seek shelter from the flying bullets. Looney took up a crouching position behind a telephone pole. After firing, Wilmerton ran back to the south sidewalk and also hid behind a telephone pole. Looney fired five times; Wilmerton four.

Others on the downtown streets and nearby businesses scrambled for cover as the two screamed threats at each other. One of Looney's shots went through an office window, narrowly missing a young woman. Workers at The Journal were horrified and rushed out the rear into the alley. Several of Wilmerton's shots struck the pole Looney hid behind. One, it was later discovered, found its mark.

Wilmerton stopped firing first and entered his office.

Pop — Looney fired a parting shot as he ran across the street just west of Wilmerton's office. Witnesses said the shootout was a blur — lasting about three minutes.

Looney walked down the street, emptying his revolver of discharged shells. After reloading, he straightened his hat and started back toward Wilmerton's office but police stopped and arrested him first. Police asked Looney for his gun. He was defiant and refused, yet followed them to the police station where the gun was taken from him.

Police found Wilmerton waiting in his office with a loaded revolver. He surrendered.

It was not initially believed that either had been wounded. Only after Looney complained to Chief L.V. Eckhart about how police had treated him was it learned he had been shot.

"Eckhart, are you going to stand for this?" demanded Looney. "Will you allow the officers to arrest and hold me without warrant, when I was shot in the back?"

"You will stay here until I investigate the case," the chief replied. "Your word is no better than Wilmerton's."

Looney lashed back with a warning. "This is an awful situation, but it isn't ended yet. The graft in this town is awful, and the only way they can stop me is to shoot me in the back and put me in the cemetery."

Dr. G.G. Craig, Sr. examined Looney and determined he had an entrance and exit wound, but that no organs had been hit.

"I cannot tell from the nature of the wounds whether Looney was shot in the back or not. There are two penetrations, the bullet entering one and passing out the other," said Dr. Craig. The wounds were about three inches apart.

Looney's News would report that he was shot in the back on his way to a meeting at the Safety Building. "He felt the sting of the bullet in the back of his hip striking the bone and then glanced off coming (out) four inches from where it went in. He turned immediately and saw Wilmerton east of him out in the middle of the street still coming towards him.

"Then the yellow streak which predominates in this rustic pervert's nature, obtained complete mastery over him and finding that his attempt to sneak up behind Mr. Looney and shoot him down had failed, and that he himself had become the target for a few bullets, he turned and ran for his office, stumbling over himself," Looney's News reported.

The confrontation was not the first attempt to silence Looney. Not long after the explosion at The News, a shot was fired at him from behind a tree. Looney, scratched by the bullet, fell from the buggy in which he was riding. Later, as Looney stood by the dining room window of his Bel Air mansion, a man jumped from behind a tree and shot and wounded him. Blood stains remained for years on the wood floor of the dining room as a reminder of the shooting. Whenever Looney would stand at the window and look out over the picturesque river valley, he would remember the surprise attack. Looney said Wilmerton was the shooter both times, but it was never proven.

In June 1909, The News told about an "assassination attempt" on Looney just after 10 o'clock on a Saturday night as Looney drove his buggy home from his law office.

"When he came under the electric light at the corner of Twelfth Avenue and Twentieth Street, he was in the full glare and readily seen by the assailants as he advanced up the Twentieth Street hill where Twelfth Street intersects it. Attempted murderer had an old make breech loading gun loaded with heavy BB shot with a heavy charge of powder and black oil cloth 2 feet by 5 feet long spread on the ground that wrapped the gun. Mr. Looney immediately fell from his buggy. He tried to raise but fell back," The News reported.

"Since W.W. Wilmerton sneaked up behind him on Third Avenue in broad daylight a few months ago, he was prepared for such an attack. He felt the shot in his left arm. Had he died on that miserable street holding the reins of his gentle horse, he would have had a prayer on his lips (to those of us who know he is deeply religious).

"Aside from the firing at about forty feet distance that struck his left arm and bruises on his fall, he is fully recovering. One shot passed through his stiff hat in the front and out the back, less than two inches from his head, another struck his arm, another lodged and entered the padding of his coat."

The rest lodged in a telephone pole on the other side of Twentieth Street. Witnesses saw one flash coming from the bushes. Two girls later found a 12-gauge shotgun in the weeds. Footprints were found in the nearby deep ravines.

"I told the captain that Wilmerton shot me," said Looney. Wilmerton was arrested the next day and bound over to the Grand Jury, but was never charged.

"It took 50 years for Abraham Lincoln's fame to be appreciated. As for myself, a less time has been required. Lincoln, unfortunately, did not have as many amateur assassins on his trail," Looney said later.

The hatred between Looney and Wilmerton would continue to simmer. But they would pale in comparison to the newspaper wars that Looney would have with The Argus up until the very end. Minnie Potter, the owner of The Argus, and son, John W. Potter, were among the well-heeled and well-connected leaders of the community. All would grow to consider Looney a cancer that needed to be removed.

Looney accused The Argus of being involved in its own underworld operation, of ruining his reputation and businesses, and of causing the death of his son. But The Argus would never back down. It steadfastly led the effort to rid Rock Island of Looney's vice organization and called for his arrest and even promoted his murder. Others would battle with Looney as well. In that era if you wrote something bad about someone, you were likely to attract bullets. Looney wrote bad things about a lot of people on a regular basis.

In September 1911, Looney's Rock Island News reported that the Schrivers, the Ramsers and one or two others were running a resort on the Rock River where men and women swam in the nude. All of this was within view of Looney's residence, which also overlooked the river and "where his children might become witness to the lewd proceedings," The News reported.

The News also went after Dina Ramser, a police matron and sister of local jeweler Jake Ramser. She drew the wrath of Looney's paper because she had been hassling the brothels protected by Looney and had the nerve to talk to the girls and help them escape. Looney's paper accused her of official misconduct.

By then Looney ruled over an extensive criminal empire.

Around noon, Thursday, September 21, 1911, Jake Ramser walked into Waddell's Barber Shop at 1825 Second Avenue, next to his jewelry store, to get a shave. He sat in one of the chairs and barber Ralph Inglehart began shaving him. John Looney walked in and sat down in the chair next to him and was shaved by Arthur Roberts. Looney got out of the chair first, followed moments later by Ramser.

"Looney, what have you got it in for me for?" Ramser asked

"Why, was there something in the paper about you?" Looney responded.

Looney pulled out a .32 caliber Colt automatic revolver, pointed it at Ramser and told him to get out of the shop. The barbers bolted — Inglehart to the cellar and Roberts behind a partition.

Ramser told Looney that he had come in the back door and was going out the same way. In saying that, he edged closer to Looney, pointed toward the door with his right hand and then grabbed Looney's gun with his left.

Looney pulled the trigger and the bullet penetrated Ramser's left hand. Ramser screamed in pain, but only became more enraged and wrestled the gun away from Looney. He threw Looney to the ground, sat on him and beat him with the butt of the gun — over and over and over again until Looney was bleeding heavily.

Ramser aimed the gun at Looney and pulled the trigger.

Click.

He aimed it at his forehead.

Click. Again. And again.

If Jake Ramser had been able to release the safety on the revolver, you probably wouldn't be reading this book today. The gun never discharged, and Ramser ended up just beating Looney with the butt of the gun — 15 or 20 times.

"He gave me an awful beating and when he got done with this, tried three times to shoot me — snapping the trigger three times in my face, but the revolver would not work," Looney said after the incident, as Dr. W.D. Snively dressed his wounds.

Looney cried for help from the large crowd that had gathered by the shop. No one stepped forward. Ramser demanded that Looney take back what he had said about him and his family, and he did.

As Looney started to regain his feet, Ramser kicked his knees out from under him and told him that all of the people hadn't heard him. "Say it loud enough for everyone to hear," he demanded.

"He continued to tell me to take back what I said in my paper and then held me down on the floor while he examined the gun in an effort to get it to work. He then pulled the trigger again, but it would not fire and he let me up," said Looney.

Looney grabbed for the gun, but Ramser put it in his coat pocket. The blood was running down Looney's face and matted in his hair, Ramser's hand was covered with blood as well.

Looney rushed out of the door, bleeding from the nose and mouth, his clothes covered with blood. He rushed to his office and grabbed another revolver. He was intercepted by Dan Drost, who brought him back to his office where the doctor tended to him while Looney drank a glass of warm milk. Looney had four cuts on the head and was bleeding profusely.

After treatment, Looney retreated to his farm on the Rock River to recover. Ramser was treated by Dr. Carl Bernardi. He later said he knew nothing about the workings of an automatic revolver, but he now had one that he was going to turn over to authorities. The two would remain arch enemies, and their hatred would play a major roll in Looney's future.

Looney abandoned his scandal sheet in 1912 after another beating at the hands of Mayor Harry M. Schriver of Rock Island. He fled to New Mexico, where he lived for nine years. But The News was revived in 1916 by Drost. In 1920, Drost and Harry M. Hamilton went to jail for a year after being convicted of libel for stories written in The News.

On March 26, 1921, big headlines in The News proclaimed: "John Looney Is Back. Dan Drost Goes To Jail." Looney and Drost, who had been a trusted lieutenant, had a falling out.

"He cobbed me out of my safety box at the bank," said Drost. The crime left him broke.

"His fangs are poisonous. He will get you, so stay away from him," Drost said of Looney.

The feud between the Drost and Looney escalated until they met in a gun battle at Market Square.

# A good whippin'

John Looney regularly used The Rock Island News to slur and libel leading citizens of the city whom he considered his enemies. Over time the "kill fees" paid to keep damaging stories out of his newspaper became quite a source of income for Looney. With some, he just enjoyed tarnishing their reputation. While most people knew that the stories in The News seldom included even a glimmer of truth, that didn't stop the vile attacks and the anger they caused.

*Mayor Harry M. Schriver*

Generally, Looney was content to focus his attacks on the city's leading newspaper, The Argus, working in frequent personal jabs along the way. Then in 1912, Looney's Irish anger got the better of him, and he used his newspaper to attack Rock Island Mayor Harry M. Schriver. Looney had pressed Schriver not to prosecute one of his crime lieutenants, Anthony Billburg, on gambling charges. When Schriver refused, Looney attacked him in several articles in The News.

A 2-inch headline cried "SCHRIVER'S SHAME" and the secondary headline accused the mayor of spending "Night and Day in Peoria in Filthy Debauch with Ethel."

On Friday, March 22, 1912, Schriver responded by arresting Looney and closing down his newspaper. He was brought to the police station, where the mayor beat Looney so severely he required hospitalization. He suffered a broken nose, four deep wounds to the head, and had blood gushing from his right ear.

*Ethel*

"Driven beyond the limit of human endurance by a libelous, defaming and besmirching attack which appeared this morning in John Looney's News, Mayor H.M. Schriver stopped, to a certain degree, the sale of the sheet, caused the arrest of 18 newsboys who were offering it for sale, and of Looney himself, and one of his henchmen, Dan Drost," The Argus reported.

Schriver said it had been "noised about" by Looney and his henchmen that the edition of the newspaper would contain the scandal sensation of the year, and men were advised to have their nickels ready. Schriver put in motion a plan to stop the widespread distribution of the paper. Warrants were prepared and officers given their instructions in advance. At 10 o'clock, Looney himself was arrested on Second Avenue by officers Kinney, Fitzsimmons and Gruby, and taken to the police station.

Schriver was beside himself with indignation. He paced the floor of the police station, the wooden floor boards creaking as he waited to confront Looney. Soon Schriver saw him in the police station with no one else in the room, according to Argus accounts. He could not control himself any longer and attacked him.

Outside the door, Looney was heard to shriek at the top of his voice, "Murder, murder. He's murdering me."

He continued to cry out until he sank to the floor after the uproar had subsided, The Argus reported.

"Listen to me, John Looney. If you ever use my name in your scandalous, blackmailing sheet again, in a scandalous article attacking my character, I will shoot you on sight! Apologize," Schriver said.

"I do, I do," Looney was heard to say, quaking.

"Apologize again," the mayor demanded, and Looney complied.

A subdued drone was heard coming from the room, believed to be Looney talking. Schriver was heard to offer one final warning.

The door opened and officers were admitted. Blood covered Looney's hands, his coat and other clothing. The wooden floor of the office was gory, and Looney's person also gave evidence of the beating as he was led to a cell. Looney asked to apologize again to Schriver and was allowed. He offered to print a special edition to retract the story. Schriver rejected the offer.

That was the story in The Argus. Looney came off as less repentant in his paper's account, although The News stories were seldom rooted in truth.

The News reported that Looney was brought to the police station and was facing the desk sergeant while he was searched. As soon as it was determined he didn't have a gun, he turned his head away from Schriver and the mayor struck him over the head with a leather-covered blackjack, "cutting a gash four inches in length into my skull and practically fracturing it," Looney claimed.

Schriver hit him two more times in quick succession.

"Take that, you dirty … die you dog. Die," Schriver reportedly said.

The third blow knocked Looney's hat from his head. Six policemen were in the room with drawn clubs.

"What is in John Looney's skull formation that made him able to withstand even these three blows first dealt him by this mayor assassin? They were fearful blows, blows intended to fell him to unconsciousness. Those blows were to be the beginning of a sure, final windup of John Looney's earthly career, for had he lost consciousness he would certainly have been beaten to death," said the story in The News.

"A scuffle ensued. I grabbed the mayor's arm, I was beaten by every one of those six strapping policemen and they used blackjacks on me," Looney claimed in his account. "Even the desk sergeant decided to lean over the rail and hit me with a blackjack. When the desk sergeant topped me on the head with a loaded weapon, I went to the floor. But before I fell, I had taken the blackjack away from the mayor. The mayor jumped on my back and choked me. Other policemen had hit me with their blackjacks. I shook the mayor off my back and broke his grip on my neck."

When Looney first saw himself in a locked room, with curtains drawn, he felt that it was a murder plot and that he would probably never come out alive. "He saw this not only by the unfolding plans but by the cruel, desperate look on the faces about him. It was a chamber of death," The News reported.

"Murder, murder. Help, help," John Looney yelled with a voice that reverberated through the building and out on the street. When Looney wrestled the blackjack from the hands of the mayor, two of the policemen standing at the doors joined the assault, according to The News, and "belted him with their clubs and bore down on his back in the corner of the room.

"He was pounded across the knuckles and wrist with a billy until the blackjack fell from his grasp and at the same time Schriver got down and proceeded to choke him, pressing his thumbs violently into his throat with all his might. As evidence of the murderous desperation with which Schriver rammed his fists into Mr. Looney's throat, his neck today, after a week's time, is swollen to nearly double its normal size and is frightfully lacerated and sore."

The News reported that while the officers were taking the blackjack from him, Looney was able to jerk one of Schriver's hands from his throat and rise up onto his feet and resume his cries for help.

"He ran first toward one door and then another, but at each door he was met with a club blow and a push to the center of the room, where he was dealt further blows from the blackjack that had been restored to Schriver," The News reported. "When Schriver was beating Mr. Looney with this instrument of death and he was yelling 'murder' and 'help' he turned to these inhuman brutes in city taxpayer uniforms and cried, 'Can't you help me? Can't you protect me? Why don't you stop this?' and these wretches stood there unmoved," The News reported.

"No, not one of these men had the heart or courage to say a word, but on the contrary let this go on for nearly an hour in that room, until the floor was like the floor of a slaughter house. Where Mr. Looney dropped on his knee, his underwear today shows a solid blood patch ten inches long where the blood on the floor soaked through his trousers and into his underwear. This floor literally ran with blood, and at the conclusion of this affair, the blood had to be removed with a mop and pail," Looney's paper reported.

"Mr. Looney was covered with it. It ran down over his collar, covering his shirt bosom, soaking his vest and the collar of his coat. It ran into his shoes until his feet were wet with blood. Schriver shed no blood of his own, but he was bloody from head to foot from contact with his victim. This awful scene, citizens, went on in your police station, in your city hall, with your mayor as the intending murderer."

According to The News version, after Looney tried to rush the doors, he went to the east side thinking he could leap through a window, but the desk sergeant intercepted him with a blow from his club that dropped him to the floor.

"Mr. Looney by this time was greatly weakened by the loss of blood and Schriver got him down in the narrow space between the sergeant's desk and the east wall and now for the first time began pummeling Mr. Looney with his fists. The mayor was now beginning to lose his wind. He puffed like a porpoise. His blows grew weaker and weaker. Finally, after thumping Mr. Looney in the face for a spell, he ordered the police to take him into what is called the bull pen or tramp room."

A blood trail marked the path as he was dragged from the room where he was beaten, down the corridor to the bull pen.

The News reported that police had left the hallway unguarded, but it flashed through Looney's mind that if he tried to make an escape they would have an excuse to shoot him. So he remained in the bull pen, pleading for air, water and a doctor.

Looney received a cup of dirty water. He touched the water to his lips, and it was bitter.

"Mr. Looney, without knowing what was in store for him, had the presence of mind to reject this water which, if not poisoned, at least tasted to him as if it contained arsenic," said The News.

After Schriver had washed off some of the blood, he called Jake Ramser on the telephone. Ramser had been in a fight with Looney several months earlier at Waddell's Barber Shop.

"Come on down Jake and see our man. Yes, come down and take a look at him," said Schriver.

After Ramser arrived, The News reported that Looney was taken into the corridor. He was so weak that he had to hang on to the wall to keep from falling.

"When I saw Ramser come into the room and the doors locked, each policeman taking his position the same as had been done in the sergeant's room, I then gave up all hope," said Looney. "I remembered how Ramser had snapped the Colt automatic over my forehead and over my heart, how he tried in every way possible to shoot me to death as I lay helpless in the barber shop. I knew now that my life was gone unless the people outside got in," Looney told The News.

Ramser approached Looney and, using vile language, declared he would now complete the job he began at Waddell's Barber Shop. Ramser started toward Looney as if to choke him.

"Jake stand back. I'm going to finish him."

*Dr. Joseph DeSilva*

Just as Schriver raised his blackjack, citizens poured into the adjoining room where they could see what was going on, according to The News' version. Looney was taken from the corridor into a small office. He asked again that Dr. Bradford be summoned. Dr. Craig soon arrived but said he could not stay. Dr. DeSilva arrived and Looney agreed to his treatment. A warrant was read to Looney and he was released on his own recognizance and taken to St. Anthony's Hospital by Dr. DeSilva, where he was operated on.

The mayor never apologized for his attack. Far from it.

"I have been driven beyond the limit of human endurance. That's all," Shriver said after the incident. "Looney has said he would get even for my prosecution of Billburg and my determination to rid the town of evil. This is his method. I do not care to say any more except that I will not stand for any more of these personal, unwarranted, blackmailing attacks, which have occurred with great frequency. Looney's animus toward me, dating back to the time I became mayor, is due to the fact that he cannot control or command me. It is merely another evidence of his attitude toward any one who he cannot use.

"The city is full of people who have been the victims of his onslaughts," the mayor said after the beating. "For my own part, it has gone as far as it can. Looney understands that."

The newsboys pleaded guilty to selling an indecent newspaper. Myron Jordan, who was believed to have written most of The News stories, also was arrested.

# March madness

John Looney's beating at the hand of Rock Island's mayor was quickly the talk of the town, and it was not Looney's nature to quietly slink off into the corner to lick his wounds — which were substantial. Four days later, on March 26, 1912, a large crowd gathered in Market Square. Opponents of Mayor Schriver, and associates of Looney, stirred the crowd. The angry mob stormed the police station and police fired back, killing two bystanders and wounding nine others.

"Officers Driven Off Streets and Trapped in Headquarters by Howling Mob. Station Showered with Missiles and All Windows in Building Smashed" headlines in The Argus read on March 27.

The riot began with a speech by E.E. Gardner, editor of the Tri-City Labor Review and socialist candidate for supervisor, who addressed a gathering in Market Square about an effort to recall the mayor.

"I feared trouble last night and during yesterday talked with various citizens as to the best and wisest course to pursue," Mayor Schriver said the next day. "I did not want to interfere with free speech, but was anxious to prevent disturbance and violence."

Schriver had a pleasant talk with Gardner, who he thought to be the only speaker scheduled, and urged him to "refrain from making inflammatory utterances. I told him to go ahead with his plans for the recall if he saw fit and to say what he pleased about my administration or official acts, but to keep within the rational lines in what he had to say."

Gardner said he had no intention of causing a disturbance. "I was very careful in my speech to urge respect for the law," he said.

Looney, however, had stacked the deck against law and order.

The purpose of the meeting was to spread fliers calling for the recall of Mayor Schriver and Commissioner Archie Hart, citing the mayor's actions in the Looney beating as cause for the recall. But when a call for a collection to finance the recall was made, the crowd of about 2,000 began to thin. When the crowd was asked to hold up their hands if they approved of the recall, only a scattered few raised their hands.

Others in the crowd, planted by Looney, berated the mayor for beating up Looney and banning distribution of The News. Harry M. McCaskrin, a candidate for state's attorney backed by Looney, urged the crowd to "go to The News office and get a paper and, if the officers interfere, overpower them."

The Chicago Record Herald newspaper reported that "one hundred thugs and four professional dynamiters were on their way to Rock Island" from Muscatine, Iowa.

Few doubted that Looney was behind the action. Apparently dissatisfied with the tameness of the meeting, a group of several hundred from outside Rock Island, believed to have been organized by Looney, lined up on Second Avenue. They

## 100 Dynam ters on Way to Rock Island
## Desperadoes Ready to Battle Soldiers
## Heavy Jail Sentences for the Rioters

Major Channon issuing order to the provost sergeant.

**Mayor's Threat to Kill**

I informed him (Looney), in the excitement, that if he continued to write me up his paper in the scurrilous, scandalous and libelous manner in which he referred to me in his last issue, I would shoot him.—*Statement by Mayor Schriver*

**The Editor's Defy.**

When the Mayor was beating me he said he would kill me, if I continued to print attacks on him. The policy of my paper will not change I am fighting for a moral principle and I am going to fight to the end.—*Statement by Editor John Looney*

issue on Saturday as usu.

*The Chicago Record Herald newspaper was one of many that reported on the rioting in the streets of Rock Island.*

began pulling on trolleys, stopping cars, throwing rocks and harassing police officers. Knowing their resistance would provoke a fight, and realizing that they were heavily outnumbered, the officers ran east along the avenue. A mob followed them to city hall where eight policemen, Mayor Schriver and Commissioner Hart were waiting.

With the mob lined up across the street, Hart stepped outside the station, held up his hands and urged the crowd to be guided by reason and refrain from any attempt at injury. His remarks were drowned by a riotous cry, followed by a fusillade of bricks, The Argus reported.

Hart went back inside and urged police not to agitate the crowd. A few minutes later, officers were startled by the firing of two shots into the west wall of the station lobby. In response, police fired over the heads of the crowd, estimated at 3,000 to 4,000. The mob briefly retreated, but came back and was met by another volley into the air. It had no effect.

Police aimed the next volley into the crowd, and several were wounded. Many of the leaders were thugs imported for the occasion. Few Rock Island residents could be recognized. The mob returned fire using revolvers and threw more bricks. Every window in the police station and some in city hall were broken. Broken glass shattered and sprayed everywhere as police dove for cover. Several bullets were fired at police through the windows. Police returned the fire into the crowd only after most of the windows in the city hall and station had been broken out and a number of policemen inside had been hit with brickbats and rocks, The Argus reported.

"We stood as much as possible and then had to let go," said Chief James Brinn.

A report that someone had been killed at the Elliott Saloon drew the mob away

*The Rock Island Argus reported that the city was under martial law.*

for a few minutes, although it was later reported that no one had been killed after all. When it returned, the efforts of the mob were doubled. When another man was reported killed on Third Avenue, some of the less reckless members of the mob left. When a third death was reported, the fight was about over, The Argus said.

The police were reinforced by Sheriff O.L. Bruner and three deputies armed with revolvers and rifles. The officers withstood the onslaught of the mob for more than one hour. By 11 o'clock, the fight was practically over and almost everyone had moved away from the station. Police only arrested three men that night.

*Sheriff
O.L. Bruner*

The sheriff contacted Governor Charles Deneen, who declared martial law and sent in National Guard troops to quell the riots. Units in Rock Island, Moline, Geneseo and Sterling were immediately mobilized. Four companies of the Sixth Regiment, about 100 men, were on duty in Rock Island the next morning. Units from Monmouth and Galesburg joined them later.

"Bayonets and swords have brought a brief period of surface tranquility in heat-ridden Rock Island's civic volcano," wrote Ray M. Leek of the Chicago Record Herald. "A score of powder men, workers in high explosives, were found skulking in a railroad yard tonight and arrested. A cool sharpshooter who fired into the city hall from a roof on a neighboring building implanted a bullet within a few feet of Mayor Schriver's head this morning."

From 3 o'clock in the afternoon until late at night, company after company were unloaded from special trains and marched to improvised barracks in the city. Groups of soldiers, outfitted in full battle gear, patrolled city streets or were strategically stationed on street corners around town. Unmistakable in dark fatigues, pants tucked into boots laced up mid-calf, wide-brimmed hats pulled down — the Guard troops did not smile and clearly meant business. They were ready for action; guns locked and loaded.

There was an uneasy tension in the air.

"With the notice that soldiers were coming, the rioters began dispersing though the streets were alive with people all night. There were various minor outbreaks and gatherings but, whenever the soldiers put in an appearance, quiet was restored at once," The Argus reported. When the riot was over, Market Square resembled a battlefield. All gatherings were outlawed and citizens were warned to keep off the streets. The mayor issued an order closing all saloons. Prostitution houses were raided and closed. Thirty-four people were arrested in the two days after the riot.

"That police did not meet violence with violence sooner is something which surprises those who knew to what humiliation they were subjected, by taunts, not to mention the missiles from the crowd assembled on the streets," The Argus reported the next day.

*In this newspaper photo, soldiers take those to jail who were charged with disturbing the peace in the days following the riots.*

Two died as a result of the riot. Frank H. Kellogg, 36, of Davenport, had come to Rock Island with his wife to watch the activities, not to participate. Raymond Swingle, 18, of 1308 44th Street, Rock Island, was downtown doing an errand for his mother when struck by a bullet in the stomach. Before dying, he told his father that he was ignored by the crowds because they thought he was faking.

Lee Fawcett, 30, was shot through the neck but the bullet missed the jugular vein. Edward Anderson of Rock Island was also seriously injured. William Heuck, 38, a resident of Rock Island, was shot in the hip. Frank Vogele, 23, was shot over the left kidney while standing on Third Avenue viewing the body of another man who had been shot. Dr. Alfred E. Stocker of Rock Island was shot in the hand while attending to a patient. Charles Johnson of Rock Island also suffered a slight flesh wound, and Herman Sackey, Alderson Dove, Nathan Harris, Edward Coleman and Joseph Eberts, all of Rock Island, also reported slight injuries. Several in the crowd were struck by birdshot.

After calm was restored, the mayor remained defiant.

"It is deplorable, but we are not going to quit now until we restore order and rid the city of the elements of disorder and defiance. Further public assemblages where political addresses may be made will not be allowed until quiet is restored, and the saloons of the city will be closed for the present," the mayor said. He was true to his word, for a while at least. The red light district was also closed.

"Not only are we going to rid the city of all men who we know are doing the city no good, but also we are going to drive these women out of the city ... We are going to clean out the bad element and, after the soldiers are gone, if it requires 50 police to do the work, it is going to be done. It is not a matter of getting money from the fines the prostitutes pay, but a matter of cleaning the city once and for all," said Commissioner Hart.

Quiet returned to the city the next night with more than 800 soldiers now patrolling the streets. Scores of people were jailed for being out on the streets after being told to leave. "Move on, you cannot stop here," was the general order. Some were arrested for shouting insults at the soldiers.

A special Grand Jury was named to investigate the riot and its cause. By the weekend, patrols had been reduced and saloons reopened from 5 a.m. to 8 p.m. By Monday, Guardsmen were being withdrawn.

At the same time, it was reported that federal agents were seeking Looney and that he might be jailed for sending libelous materials through the mails. But Looney was long gone, having left town to recuperate from his beating. He would return nine years later, in March 1921, to re-establish control over vice in Rock Island.

In the interim, he would visit both Rock Island and Ottawa periodically, sometimes slipping in and out of town unannounced or in disguise. In March 1919, he returned to Ottawa for the funeral of his 83-year-old mother, Margaret. He had long-since skimmed anything of value from her. While he lived a life of opulence, she spent her final years living in poverty at St. Joseph's Convent in Ottawa, where she died after a long illness.

She was buried at St. Columba Cemetery in an unmarked grave.

# Home on the range

In March 1912, with the city of Rock Island under marshal law following the Market Square riots, John Looney was whisked out of town by auto to Ottawa, where he had many friends and family. There he lay low, recovered from his beating and plotted the direction his life would take.

As had been the case since he was young, John Looney felt the call of the West. The first time he left Ottawa as a teenager, he got only as far as Rock Island. This time, his journey took him all the way to the Wild West, where he visited his brother Jerry in Colorado and Tim in Albuquerque, New Mexico. John fell in love with the West, as he knew he would, while bouncing around visiting family and friends.

Late in 1913, while on a duck-hunting trip out of Monero, New Mexico, with an Indian guide, John Looney discovered a dramatic and isolated area in northwest New Mexico that he decided to call home. By early in 1914, Looney had purchased more than 20,000 acres of land near Horse Lake, adjacent to the Apache Indian reservation, and began a new career as a rancher.

"I saw this sunny country and became taken with it and began negotiations for the purchase of the ranch," said Looney.

Horse Lake Ranch was located at an elevation of about 7,000 to 8,000 feet. Looney used the area south of Horse Lake to raise cattle and sheep. A mile below the lake was the main house, surrounded by three wooden sheds and a handler's house. Three miles south of that was a second house and still further south, a third. It was 25 miles to the nearest railroad or telegraph office and 10 miles to the nearest neighbor. It was a perfect location for Looney to cook up his illegal operations without anyone knowing what he was up to. The ranch was located in Rio Arriba County near Chama, New Mexico.

Looney's land was populated in some areas by evergreen forests and elsewhere with scattered juniper and pinion. There was Ponderosa pine, and white and red cedar, but predominately the land was covered with grasses: blue gramma, galleta, wheatgrass, rice grass, wild clover and dryland alfalfa, along with sagebrush and rabbit brush. Mostly there were rocks — a lot of rocks.

Looney's career as a rancher was about as successful as every other lawful enterprise he tried. At times, he would buy stock in the fall, only to have it killed off by the harsh high-country winters. At other times, Looney wouldn't feed the animals, or they would wander away. At horse and cattle auctions, Looney looked almost like a comic book character with his pants tucked into his boots, but with one leg sometimes hanging down. He would wear a stylish western shirt, but with it hanging out of his pants; a huge, over-sized western hat and an oversized neckerchief pulled up to his chin. He was quite a sight.

Newspaper accounts of the time painted a picture of Looney as a failed rancher. It was reported that every spring he would ship in thousands of dollars worth of blooded stock, only to allow them to freeze and starve to death the following winter. At one time, he shipped in 13 train cars of cattle, at an estimated value of more than $100,000. Ranchers in New Mexico did not hold Looney, the quality of his stock, or his operation in high esteem. The few head that had survived the hardship of winter were inbred to the point of destroying their value.

"His high-handed methods made him disliked by most of the ranchmen with property near his, and his disregard for the courtesies of the country made his ranch one to be avoided," The Rock Island Argus reported. "A reckless use of guns, even in a land where gunplay is usually not a thing to create excitement, characterized many of his actions and further helped to develop among the natives an apathy to even going near the canyon in the Apache Reservation which houses his ranch."

One area that Looney might have excelled in was raising racehorses. Of course, his purpose was to race them and gamble. At one point, Looney was handling a bronco and was severely injured by a kick in the face. He was hospitalized, and it was said he might die; he didn't, and his legend continued to grow.

Back in Rock Island, it was assumed that Looney had simply fled to New Mexico, but the fact was that he never stayed long in one place. He was constantly traveling to Colorado, California, Kansas City, Texas and even Mexico. He would also take trips back to Illinois where he would visit Ottawa, or steal into Rock Island unannounced. Frank Hobbs, deputy sheriff of Ft Worth, Texas, once said Looney was as infamous in Texas as he was in Rock Island. His trips were often to race or gamble on horses, or to search for a

*Looney's ranch wasn't much more than rocks and brush. The Beauchamp family lived for a while at the ranch in 1919-1920. Roberta Beauchamp, right, and an unidentified friend play with a lamb. Sisters Bessie and Eleanor Beauchamp are in the background. Outbuildings were very modest.*

*The Beauchamp children, from left, Eleanor, Bessie and Roberta, are shown near a pond on the Looney ranch in New Mexico. Photo is from about 1920.*

poker game. Along the way, he made new contacts with other nefarious individuals who would later play a role in his crime empire. The cities he visited, while he was thought to be in "exile" in the southwest, would actually become sources and destinations for horseracing, women, drugs and stolen autos.

His son, Connor, lived with him in New Mexico during this time, while his daughters attended school in Rock Island at the Villa de Chantel. Kathleen Looney, who graduated from the school in 1912, was the business manager of Days and Deeds, the yearbook published by the students. Both Kathleen and Ursula were involved in plays at the school. Ursula was also involved in athletics and the Literary Club. After graduation, Kathleen would leave to become a nun in St. Louis.

Looney's ranch was the perfect getaway. It was so remote, no one ever knew if he was there or not, and in the winters it was often inaccessible, when snows four to eight feet deep could bury the region. When snow is waist-deep, with howling winds often causing drifts twice as high and making it impossible for even birds to travel, folks weren't likely to venture out, much less try and sneak up on Looney. Deputy sheriff Hobbs called the ranch "the safest place in the world."

As isolated as he was, Looney still had run-ins with the law and with neighbors. His ranch was located in an area that was considered open range, where cattle could be driven across private property. One time, cattle of Mrs. H.C. Turrell of Durango, Colorado, who owned the adjoining ranch, wandered onto Looney's property, so he claimed them. When Mrs. Turrell came near his ranch in search of the cattle, Looney shot at her, but he was often known to take shots at interlopers. In 1923, he was also wanted for cattle rustling. Of course, the life of a rancher worked in reverse, too. Sometimes Looney's cattle would wander off or other ranchers would help hurry them away. In most cases, Looney never even knew they were gone.

Also known to disappear were some of Looney's workers, who often went unpaid for long periods of time. In 1922, Mrs. Elmer Johnson reported that her son had left Rock Island about a year before to work for Looney on his ranch in New Mexico. He disappeared and later was reported to have died. His body was later found on the Looney ranch — apparently he had been murdered.

Eleanor Beauchamp Peterson remembers living on Looney's ranch in about 1919. They had been living in Rock Island, but her father made arrangements to do carpentry work on the New Mexico ranch. "My parents had been told there would be arrangements made for schooling, but this never materialized," she recalled.

"I was about four and our family consisted of my father, mother, a younger sister about two and an older sister about seven. We had playmates in New Mexico and they had dark hair and dark skin, and we girls had light hair and light skin. We were restricted to designated areas because there were places with quicksand not far away. I do remember that there were no grassy areas for play, just plain dirt."

The children were left to play in the dirt while Looney plotted his criminal empire.

"Sometime during our stay in New Mexico, my older sister remembers there had been shots fired, but no one had been hit. I do not recall a personal encounter with Looney, but my father had concerns that all was not right. Several enemies of Looney had disappeared on his ranch, never to be seen again. Some people mentioned quicksand. One night my father left and walked to the nearest town and brought back help for our departure, and we moved to Denver, Colorado," said Mrs. Peterson.

By 1917, Looney had begun making regular appearances in Rock Island again, but often as a shadowy figure moving quickly in and out of town. In his

*Dan Drost*

absence, Looney's former crime lieutenants, Anthony Billburg and Dan Drost, and a few city officials had taken control of vice in the city. For some time, Billburg had been a loyal and feared enforcer for the Looney organization, but with his former boss out of town, Billburg had decided to take charge. On March 26, 1921, headlines in the Rock Island News proclaimed "Looney is Back" and "Dan Drost Goes to Jail." Looney was back, and his goal was to re-establish control over vice in Rock Island and the region.

It was the jailing of Drost that spurred Looney's return to Rock Island. Drost had earlier shut down publication of The News for several months while he visited Looney at his ranch in New Mexico and convinced him to let Harry M. Hamilton run The News, with Drost as the news gatherer. In reality, Drost was only doing the bidding of Anthony Billburg, who really was in control. Looney agreed, but because Drost was generally an illiterate man, Looney enrolled his daughter, Ursula, to write for the paper until she left Rock Island for college. After she left, Drost found others to write for him.

World War I had begun, the Rock Island Arsenal was bustling, wages were high and money was plentiful. Circulation of The News went up, and Drost thought he was the reason for the paper's success. He became arrogant, reckless and soon did not care who he wrote about or what he wrote. The result was that Drost and Hamilton soon found themselves jailed for libel. Looney tried to advise Drost, but Drost thought he knew more than Looney, would not listen and became abusive. When Looney found out he had been tricked and that Drost and Billburg had control of his paper, he was furious. He decided it was time to wrestle back control of The News.

So John Looney got tough, returned to his old tricks, cranked up his printing press and went on the offensive. Billburg and Drost started a rival paper, the Tri-City Journal, and every article attacked Looney.

"This character tries to tell you he is trying to rid the community of The News. Who are his associates in the venture? Here we have one George Buckley, proprietor of a gambling house and house of prostitution, a bootlegging joint and dope fiend; Anthony Billburg, so notorious in crime that the mention of his name is synonymous with crime, and 'Kid' Warner and Monte McCall, members of the old (Mabray) Gang and Jim Darnell, a sore-head and hanger-on in Rock Island for many years," Looney wrote in The News. "Now, citizens, what do you think of a gang like this cleaning up the city of Rock Island? Why the stench from a sewer is but perfume compared to the smell that emanates from such carrion. Do the vultures think they can pull the wool over your eyes with this kind of rot? No one but ignoramuses like Drost and the bunch behind him would attempt such tactics ..."

Not only did Looney reclaim The News, perhaps the cornerstone of his crime empire, he also reasserted control over many other illegal operations that had fallen under the control of Billburg and other rival gangs in his absence. In 1921, Lowell H. "Cy" Hazlett, a pimp with morals lower than a snake who ran a bawdy house called the Rex Hotel next to The Argus newspaper, became co-publisher of The News with Looney. As a young man, illness caused Hazlett's mother to send him to New Mexico where he worked for the railroad and had an accident from which both his legs were amputated. At The News, he first worked with Drost and later Looney and became totally familiar with the paper's operations. Eventually he became more proficient at writing and penned much of what was published in the paper. Tom Cox, the city's crooked police chief, also part of the Looney crime ring, would give Hazlett the names of people involved in compromising situations to be written up.

When Drost got out of jail, he went after Looney to get money he claimed he was owed for keeping the paper in publication. Drost said Looney owed him several thousand dollars for running the business and collecting money for him while Looney was out of town. But Drost had not told Looney that he was working for Billburg, and had diverted funds to Billburg's organization.

Looney had no intentions of paying Drost a dime. He set him up in a land-sale scam that the uneducated Drost fell for. Looney took Drost for every cent he had in the bank, plus the money that he supposedly owed him. Looney's daughter, Ursula, helped with the scam, and when it was over, she emptied a lock box full of cash as Drost haplessly stood by and watched. Drost, now broke, joined the growing list of Looney-haters.

By this time, Rock Island had 16 square blocks of vice that included and surrounded the city police station. Brothels, chop suey houses, assignation houses, cribs, saloons, dance halls and cabarets spread from Second Avenue south on Ninth Street and across Third and Fourth Avenues east to 24th Street. Like the city's legitimate economy, it was fueled by a transportation crossroads where two rivers, several key roads and many railroads converged. This district provided work to scores of people as well as income to officials who were on the take. The red light district showed amazing profits, and the police and politicians had their hands out-stretched. The amounts of "protection" money extorted from businesses was huge and provided immunity from prosecution from judges, prosecutors, the mayor, chief of police and lawyers, all of whom got a cut. The money from corruption was immeasurable and extended from the cop on the beat to the mayor.

Rock Island's trains, railroad yards, hotels and steamboats kept customers pouring into the city in search of its notorious women, booze and gambling. Row after row of taverns and cheap hotels were scattered throughout the city — all within walking distance of each other. Whatever people wanted, Rock Island had to offer. Everyone benefited — from beauty parlors, hotel owners and doctors, to bartenders, waiters, cab drivers and lawyers.

In it John Looney only saw opportunity. The timing of his return couldn't have been better. Rock Island vice exploded in 1920 fueled by Prohibition. This time around, Looney's former foes, including Mayor Harry Schriver and Police Chief Thomas Cox, would become allies. Looney's criminal operation would include bootlegging as far north as Wisconsin and south into Missouri. He operated brothels and gambling parlors throughout the region and beyond, and an auto-theft ring that stretched across the United States.

Helen Van Dale, his madam and second only to Looney in the crime syndicate, controlled more than 300 girls who were distributed throughout the Midwest. They even supplied girls to Chicago gangster Johnny Torrio.

Looney also engaged his son, Connor, then 18, in his illegal activities.

Looney soon controlled almost all of the gambling and prostitution houses, which one count put at about 150. He collected payoffs for protection from local businesses. But in the most ironic twist of all, the payoffs paid for protection from the police, because Looney also controlled them, along with the mayor and police chief.

Looney still enjoyed a game of cards himself, but couldn't even gamble fair and square. One old-time resident remembered Looney showing up for a poker game with some Greeks in Rock Island. He lost, but then demanded his money back. They ran him off. He threatened to write them up in his newspaper, and they laughed — but they were probably laughing at his outfit. He showed up wearing his oversized western cowboy hat, black tailed coat, a bandana around his neck, cowboy boots and two pearl-handled revolvers in leather holsters.

Emeal Davis, an enormous black man, replaced Tony Billburg as Looney's bodyguard and "muscle" after Billburg started his own organization. Davis himself owned several houses of prostitution and nightclubs. He wasn't as tough as Billburg, but was twice as dangerous. He thrived on violence and was acquainted with the vilest criminals in the underworld. He would follow any orders given to him by Looney, so if Looney needed a nasty job done, Davis was the man.

Transporting girls and illegal booze was his specialty. Davis used Looney's boat to drop cases of bootleg whiskey at designated towns along the Mississippi River corridor from Dubuque to Keokuk and often even farther. He had men he could trust to load and unload the docks, and the toughest men he could find were on board to keep the peace. He also delivered stolen cars to as far away as Kansas City and New Mexico.

Davis was also responsible for obtaining weapons for the Looney organization's arsenal. Shot guns, rifles, hand guns, knives, black jacks, brass knuckles and even hand grenades were stored in Looney's Bel Air barn and his "Roost" on the hill. Davis was a menacing presence to Looney's enemies, but friendly and humorous to his friends.

Looney's relationship with Davis would later develop complications. A centerpiece in Looney's operation was a large launch named "Marithia," which he kept at LeClaire, Iowa. The boat was used to haul booze up and down the Mississippi River. Looney also used it for quick getaways. But in 1922, Davis, who said Looney owed him $1,250, went to LeClaire and took possession of the boat in an attempt to get his money. According to some reports, Davis planned to anchor the boat in the river and start a gambling resort there. When Davis learned it would be a violation of federal law, he abandoned the plan and instead pulled out the stopcocks and sank the boat.

# Kick the devil out

With crime exploding in 1919, and Looney starting to reappear again regularly, community leaders in Rock Island sought to bring a leading evangelist to town to help clean up the corruption. When the Reverend William Ashley "Billy" Sunday arrived on an autumn afternoon in September, the devil- and rum-fighting icon vowed to go after black-hearted gangsters in the area then known as the Tri-Cities. As Sunday left Chicago by train, he proclaimed with anger in his voice, "I am on my way to kick the devil out of the Tri-Cities — Moline, Rock Island and Davenport."

Both Rock Island and Looney were squarely in the evangelist's sights.

"Rock Island, that Citadel of Sin, is the wickedest city in the United States of America, bar none. And the leader of that wickedness is John Patrick Looney," said Sunday.

A huge crowd gathered at the Rock Island railroad depot to greet Sunday, a former resident of a Davenport orphanage who had the joy of battle shining in his eyes. "I didn't expect such a monstrous welcome, but I might have known what I'd get because that's the way you people do things — on a hundred horse power scale if you back it up with your convictions."

Sunday was powerful in both build and presentation. He was built like an athlete — small at the waist tapering from broad, well-formed shoulders. Sunday had been a professional baseball player before becoming an evangelist. His movements were quick and supple as a cat, and he was alert to everything going on around him, quick of wit and well-prepared for any emergency. His dress was immaculate from the patent leather oxfords, silk stockings, spotless white silk shirt, white collar and small black tie, to the well-cut, tailor-made suits. "Perhaps you have noticed he's quite a dandy," wrote The Argus.

His first meeting was at 10:45 on a beautiful autumn morning, Sunday, September 14, 1919, in a tabernacle built for him on the corner of Fifth Avenue and 24th Street in Rock Island. Every protestant church in the Quad-Cities took part, canceling their Sunday morning services. "Society, booze and Bolshevism" were slammed, and the black-hearted gang of the Tri-Cities was berated with shouts and gestures by the flamboyant preacher. The crowds were estimated at 6,000 to as much as 10,000 or more for each sermon as he continued to make appearances for seven weeks. Newspapers reported his lengthy sermons, word for word. On Sunday, October 6, he drew his largest crowd yet of about 10,000, but a sermon for women only on October 25, drew 11,000.

"The devil's crowd is always hanging around. I want to tell you I know who the bunch here is, and that their end is to come quick and sudden," said Sunday.

"The old world is going to hell so fast it's breaking the speed limit," said Sunday to his now-revved up crowd. "People are playing hide and seek with God and tag with the devil."

"The liquor traffic is alive today, although reported dead. I want to tell you that the saloon is OK in its place, but that place is in hell. The dirty bunch that runs it is still active and working. If it hadn't been for some of you God forsaken church members, they'd all be in hell long ago."

In the closing words of one of his sermons, his attacks were made while standing on the pulpit, where he jumped from a chair. With one foot on the chair and the other on the rostrum, he shouted, "Come on, forces of evil in the Tri-Cities. I defy you. Come on. Come on." He challenged the churches, while blasting some as well, and waded into politics without hesitation. Then, abruptly, he broke off with, "All right, ushers, now for the offering. Let's see how the old Tri-Cities can do for us. Go to it."

"Lots of people look like they are handcuffed when the plate passes by," he mused.

By the end of his seven-week crusade, $48,923 was raised with more than $20,000 going to the preacher. The remainder covered construction of the tabernacle and other expenses. More than 10,000 pledged to convert and become Christians during the seven weeks.

Near the end of the revival campaign, Sunday said, "There are many who will be saved in the Tri-Cities, many good people here, but a large percentage are still on the downward path." In his farewell, Sunday said the community had "gotten tangled in my heart strings as few towns have before. I think some of the finest people in the country live here — and one or two of the meanest. … May the Lord continue to bless you until the day dawns and the shadows flee away."

Looney and his gang just laughed and shrugged him off. They saw Billy Sunday as a phony Bible thumper who bilked unfortunate followers the same way they did, only using emotional religious scripture to do it. Looney called him a "charlatan" who spent the public's donations for expensive cars and clothes.

In fact, the honest ministry of the area lost thousands of dollars. Billy Sunday was healing the sick and elderly with a touch of one hand to their foreheads, as he passed the collection plate with the other. Meanwhile, one block away Helen Van Dale and Jenny Mills had girls doing tricks 24 hours a day. Illegal booze was sold all night just two doors down from Sunday's meeting. In fact, the illegal joints had no locks on the doors because they never closed. That was Rock Island and the Tri-Cities in 1919.

In September 1922, Thomas B. Fowler went undercover for The Argus. He painted an even more detailed picture of life in the underworld of Rock Island. He found that bartenders poured whisky under the eyes of police officers. He reported that gin had become a favorite drink in Rock Island and was sold in most bars for 50 cents a glass. A better grade of bonded liquor could be had for 75 cents a drink.

"There are various kinds of beverages sold over the bars, but it is the whisky and gin that you are guaranteed the old-time kick that the Volstead law (Prohibition) was meant to remove as a temptation to the American people," Fowler reported in The Argus. "I would not hesitate to charge that there are more laws violated in Rock Island than there are law-abiding citizens."

Bar operators told the reporter that selling hooch openly was "all a matter of making arrangements with the fixers. They say we have an immunity ring in Rock Island." They would buy hooch from the makers at $3 per gallon and sell it to bars that were guaranteed protection for $7 or $8 per gallon. Looney, of course, was the leader when it came to both making and selling hooch whiskey — shipping it up and down the river by boat. Fowler's report estimated hundreds of gallons of hooch whiskey were sold weekly in the city's bars and houses of prostitution. He admitted to not knowing how much the crime rings collected in Rock Island, but he guessed it could easily mount into thousands of dollars each week — huge amounts for that era.

The majority of the money went to Looney, who was the best at controlling the business and collecting the fees. Looney also made the bars buy advertising in his newspaper as another part of the shakedown. One bar owner estimated that as many as six men benefited from the protection racket.

Fowler visited a bar and house of prostitution on Third Avenue and 21st Street. There, he met the woman in charge and six girls who served the men. There wasn't much business, Fowler observed, and asked one of the girls why.

"Them damned buzz wagons is putting us on the blink," answered an auburn-haired girl who said she was from Chicago. "The birds that used to spend their money with us now buy a pint of hooch and pick a flapper off the curb and go for a joy ride in the country."

Fowler remarked that he didn't suppose selling liquor was allowed.

"In Rock Island?" said a brown-haired girl who didn't look to be older than 17. "Man, you can get away with murder in this here burg if you are in right, and we are in right, take it from me."

"Things is fixed in this here town of Rock Island," continued the auburn-haired girl. "In Chicago, the coppers was always chasing us, but down here we're all setting pretty. A girl that knows her stuff can make money in Rock Island when the district is wide open. Of course, once in a while we've got to slow up, but that didn't mean anything except that we've got to lay low. When I was engaged in Chicago to come and board at this place, I was told that I could stay in Rock Island as long as I wanted to and that I'd never be pinched. The trouble in other cities is that the dicks is always running us in and getting us fined. That keeps us broke."

The businesses had no closing time. "We're open just as long as there is any money in sight," said the girl. "We're never bothered by the police. There are a couple of men you have got to see in Rock Island to get protection. I don't know what this place has to pay, but I guess it pays enough because I heard the madam kicking yesterday that she was getting tired of buying automobiles for other people that don't do anything but act as go-betweens. But you've got to give it to them, they've got the business down pretty fine."

It was about 11 o'clock when Fowler visited a bar between 22nd and 23rd streets over which a black woman seemed to be presiding with her assistant. The woman led him to the second floor where a party was in progress. "You ain't one of those government devils are you?" she asked, and he assured her he wasn't.

In the dance hall, several young white men, all well dressed, were dancing with the black women. All had been drinking hooch whisky and beer. Fowler asked one of the girls if black men ever visited. She assured him they would be bounced if they did. "We cater only to white folks, and you'd be surprised at some of the nice boys that come to visit us. Once in a while they bring their white girls with them just to show them what a dandy place we've got here," the girl said.

"I bet you're worried about your little wife right now. You just forget her for a little while. We're all nice girls even if our hide is dark," she added.

A few doors down was another black restaurant and house of prostitution. Fowler found a gathering of black women and a mixture of white and black men. This was not as high-class a resort as the first one, he noted. The women were poorly dressed, haggard and dissipated. One of the women made the usual proposal to Fowler. A black sitting at a table dropped a glass on the floor.

"That crazy coke-head. He ought to have a high chair and a bib. He's hitting too much snow. First thing he knows he'll land where there ain't none of that old stuff to be had," she said.

Fowler also visited hotels on Market Square and found prostitutes and whiskey available at all three. One of them had a gambling room with a craps table and several men playing poker. Drinks were served to the players.

"Isn't this going pretty strong for a Sunday school town?" Fowler asked a young man watching the craps game.

"Sunday school town? Hell, where do you get that stuff? Why, brother, this is nothing. You haven't seen anything. I saw a guy strong-armed here one night. He claimed he was frisked for a big roll of money, and when he hollered that he would tell the police, he was reminded that if he did, he would be locked up. This bunch around here don't care about police. If a copper came in here right now and ordered the game closed, he'd probably be ordered out on the sidewalk and the chances are he would move, too, because if he didn't, he would lose his star."

Second in power to Looney in his crime syndicate was proud and haughty Helen Van Dale, the queen of the underworld. Helen, and her sister, "Dimples," ran Looney's prostitution racket, which was considered the largest in the United States. Girls all over the country, from New Mexico to New York, came to Rock Island to work for them. Looney had many brought in from Mexico, north to Denver and then east to Iowa and Illinois. Some were younger than 17 years old.

Helen Van Dale — born Catherine Helena Lee — was stubborn as a child, and when she wanted to do something, no one could stop her. Family members said, "when Helen cracked the whip, you'd better jump." Classmates at St. Mary's School for Girls in Knoxville, Illinois, near Galesburg, remembered her as really cocky and full of herself. She was born in 1893 in Paris, Illinois, to James Perry Lee and his wife, Nancy. She had one sister, Lillie ("Dimples") and her father was but a shadowy figure in her life. Nancy moved with the girls to Galesburg when they were very young. At St. Mary's School, Helen was known as an avid reader, a mover and shaker, and a tough public speaker. She developed a real interest in Greek history, which contributed to her Helen of Troy persona.

*Helen Van Dale, Looney's "Queen of the Brothels."*

Somehow, a sleazy character who ran a saloon and brothel in Galesburg dazzled Helen with the possibility of earning large sums of money as a prostitute. There was little money available at the time, so she decided to give it a try. In a statement years later, Helen said she was 16 years old when she first sold herself for money. At age 19, she moved with Billy Rice to Rock Island to work full-time as a prostitute, and, after working for him for a while, Tony Billburg offered her a "better cut" to work at his place on 20th Street. There she met one of Billburg's bartenders named Henry Van Dale. He was married with a family, but was a tall, handsome, friendly fellow, and Helen worked her charms on him. They eventually were married and left Billburg's saloon and brothel and opened their own at 327 E. Fifth Street in Davenport, at the foot of the Arsenal Bridge. It was 1917, World War I had begun and the Arsenal was bustling. Helen's sister, "Dimples" later joined the business, not as a prostitute but keeping the books.

Helen had a roving eye and fell for a handsome, well-known local athlete, Lester "L.C." Smith. She divorced Van Dale and married Smith and moved with him to Rock Island, where she worked for the notorious madam Jennie Mills until she could open a place of her own. Despite what would become a string of marriages, perhaps as a mark of celebrity, she was always known as Helen Van Dale.

Government agents who tracked her for years described Helen as "one of the most interesting madams in the annals of prostitution." Beginning with just herself at 19 years of age, she built a stable of more than 300 girls under her control. Under Looney's protection, she became so well-known that prostitutes around the country sought her out for work. She placed them in cities in the Midwest and beyond, including providing girls for the toughest mob in the world, that of Chicago's Johnny Torrio.

No authority was strong enough to stop Helen. She told her girls that they couldn't be touched because she was "Queen of the Brothels" and would protect them. Her base of operations was Rock Island, the Citadel of Sin, where she was protected by Looney and Police Chief Tom Cox. Helen sent girls throughout the area controlled by Looney and beyond. Billy Rice, who brought her to Rock Island and owned a saloon and brothel at 2127 Fourth Avenue, now worked for Helen.

Van Dale kept her personal stock for the Tri-Cities, where she and her sister ran three places in Rock Island from 20th Street to 24th Street along Second and Third Avenues; three or four more in Davenport; and a hotel and saloon on Old Harbor Road in Nahant, west of Davenport along the Mississippi River. This included the Palmer Inn and Hollywood Inn, run by the notorious "Lil" Maloff, alias "Lil" Tank, who was an agent for Looney controlled by Van Dale.

*Notorious madam Jennie Mills ran businesses on Rock Island's 22nd Street until her death in 1958. All of the structures have since been razed.*

Her main house was on the northwest corner of 24th Street and Fourth Avenue in Rock Island — just off the bridge to the Rock Island Arsenal, a military installation that employed thousands. The entrance to her house was on Fourth Avenue, and to her bar was on 24th Street. She and her sister lived there along with a maid, Lena. "Dimples" was married to the bartender at their Rock Island place, Heinie Lee, whose real name was Victor Cielseski. If the girls needed anything, they would call Lena.

The average price paid for services was three to five dollars, with 50 percent going to the house. The girls were continually graded according to their looks and ability to make money, and Helen would move them around from place to place. Helen would greet customers at each place with a friendly "Come on in, suckers," or "How you doin' sweet cheeks?"

She defied every city, county and state official and had pictures of many of them with her girls. Once, when a prosecuting attorney asked her in court if she had been a prostitute, she snapped back, "You should know. You were in my house…"

At another case filed against some of her girls, the prosecutor asked Helen if she signed a register when she signed in with a customer. "Of course, just like I did with you when we went there." Red-faced and speechless, the prosecutor turned away. The jury roared with laughter and the judge had to hammer his gavel to restore order. As Helen's reputation grew, so did the number of "big shots" who visited her pleasure parlors and she made sure they knew her. Her activities became bolder and bolder.

The G-men credited her with building an immense white-slave ring that extended across the country. She claimed many times that she was immune to arrest, and Looney and Cox protected her by shaking down the brothel and saloon owners and paying off officials. Eventually, Cox fell for her charms, which extended her control inside the city police department. But Cox wanted Smith out of Helen's life, so he could replace him as her lover. He would harass Smith, work him over and even threw him in jail for a day or two. One time he had him brutally beaten and thrown in the back seat of his own cab.

Helen wanted Smith out of her life, too, so she could gain the power that sleeping with Chief Cox would bring, even though he had a wife and family. She claimed mental cruelty and filed for divorce from Smith.

When Van Dale was brought into the organization, it sewed up the prostitution side of Looney's vice ring. The proceeds from the girls were split three ways — between Looney, Cox and Van Dale. Blond and attractive, about 5 feet 4 inches tall, very busty, and usually wearing the latest fashions and draped with an expensive mink coat, Helen Van Dale was always confident with a merry twinkle in her eyes. But she never took crap from anyone.

Looney secretly hated Van Dale, but kept it to himself because the money just kept rolling in. He would try from time to time to frighten her, but that only made her mad. The organization was constantly scouting for new locations. When Helen found a good location, one of Looney's lieutenants, Louis Ortell, would tell him and he would purchase it for her. The organization quickly spread throughout the Midwest.

In the 1920s, Looney's crime empire had branched out to include a nationwide stolen-car ring that extended from Philadelphia, Chicago, Rock Island, Minneapolis and St. Paul and included New Mexico and old Mexico. Looney used crime contacts he had developed in other cities during his time away from Rock Island to create a ring with its center in Rock Island and the Tri-Cities. The connections also served to boost the trafficking of narcotics with men driving stolen cars to Mexico and then returning with dope to be peddled in Rock Island, until the region became a haven to addicts.

As Looney's empire grew following his return from self-imposed exile, Allan Fordney, alias "Chicago Whitey," came to Rock Island as a bodyguard for John Looney. Also added to the Looney payroll were Albert Wagner, alias Joe Kasmouski, a paroled con from Joliet and two other professional gunmen from New York. All were wanted in various cities around the country and provided muscle for the

Looney crime organization. All were professional safe crackers and holdup men and carried with them an arsenal of guns and other tools of the trade. But mostly they were trusted with the task of stealing autos and delivering them to Rock Island.

After several trips moving "hot" cars, Looney and Chicago Whitey got into a fierce argument after Looney refused to pay him. Whitey vowed he would kill Looney.

"Not if I kill you first," Looney threatened back.

Chicago Whitey and the others defected to the gang led by Billburg and Drost. But a sweeping series of arrests by federal agents and Chief Investigator M.S. Mosher of Chicago, designed to close the noose around the gangs of the local underworld, apprehended all four men in Davenport and Rock Island.

The passage of the Dyer Act in October 1919 had placed interstate transportation of stolen vehicles under federal law. When captured, they had several license plates that had been stolen. In the basement of the house they were renting were two stills, mash and skeleton keys, as well as an assortment of auto parts and accessories. Chicago Whitey admitted that Billburg and Drost had hired them to kill Looney and policemen who were impeding their crimes. The four told Rock Island County States Attorney Ben Bell where stolen autos were stored for resale in Kansas City.

Once again, John Looney had escaped impending death, but the noose was beginning to tighten.

# The gang's all here

Anthony Billburg was a hulking Swede from southern Iowa, a coal miner's son who wanted more from life than Centerville offered. He moved to Davenport, Iowa, in early 1905 and found work as a bouncer in the notorious Bucktown district, a wide-open, no-holds-barred place where gambling, prostitution, and you-name-it all existed. He worked in saloons and whore houses that were extremely dangerous. Tony Billburg was as mean as they come and not a man to fool with. His motto was, "If you pull out a gun, use it. Get them before they get you."

*Anthony Billburg*

"In a fight, I'll take Billburg," the owner of a saloon he worked in said. "You can have five other guys."

Saloon keepers and madams who hired Billburg for his terrible temper and reputation both feared and admired him. They would react with terror when he cleaned out rowdy patrons in a fight. He could do it in minutes. Once he hit a tough customer across the bridge of his nose with a ball bat; blood gushed everywhere. Billburg dragged him out to the sidewalk and nonchalantly dropped him in the gutter.

In Bucktown, no one paid attention to such tactics. The police didn't care.

Billburg also gambled with the best in the nation. Davenport was then well known from New York to California as a gambler's paradise. High rollers gathered in Bucktown for games that lasted days. Billburg was referred to as a "damn good" poker player by the experts.

Pretzel Alley was another playground for gamblers in Davenport, running between Main and Harrison between Third and Fourth streets. A whole lot calmer than wild Bucktown, it was suited to businessmen who enjoyed having a good time playing cards and downing a few drinks without brawling and excitement. There were professional types and flamboyant characters hanging out in the Alley. Tony Billburg spent his time there when he wasn't working. Most liked Billburg, and his presence was appreciated since having a well-mannered bouncer around kept the patrons comfortable. He had friends in high places who paid him big money for his services — and then lost money to him in poker games.

When the city was reformed by Mayor Harry Phillips in 1906 and '07, the regulars in Bucktown just crossed the river to Rock Island, and Billburg went along with them. Billburg had money and used it to purchase most of the block of buildings on 20th Street between Second and Third Avenues, across from the city park named Spencer Square. It was here, in 1907, that Billburg met his match in John Patrick Looney.

Billburg trusted no one, but neither did Looney. They were associates, never friends. Men like Billburg and Looney didn't have friends.

Billburg owned saloons and employed prostitutes. His wife, Margaret, was the madam, and high-stakes gambling helped fill his establishments. Billburg was a shrewd boss. His bartenders wore uniforms without pockets — nothing into which cash could be slipped. He used mirrors and hired a manager to watch them "just to keep 'em honest."

Early on, Looney was Billburg's attorney. Then they became more than associates. Billburg was Looney's intimidator and enforcer. When Looney's customers didn't pay for his protection, Tony would "smooth them over." First, there would be pressure without violence. If that didn't work, "muscle" was employed. When Looney was threatened, Billburg was his bodyguard. Only Looney held a higher position in the crime organization. When Looney left town after the 1912 riot, Billburg took over the number one spot and led the organization, despite being found guilty of gambling charges in early 1912.

Billburg was content to work for Looney, tend to his business and use his muscle as needed for the "old man." There was one problem. By now, Mayor Harry Schriver had his own protection plan and neither Looney nor Billburg fit in. Two factions, same agenda: extract donations from both legal and illegal operations.

Since Billburg was Looney's "muscle," Schriver went after him. The mayor thought Billburg was more of a threat than Looney — definitely more dangerous. Schriver used the police department to harass him. Raid and fine. Raid and fine. Again and again. The Rock Island Argus newspaper would write up Billburg as a law violator and Looney associate.

As a result, Looney went after Schriver in his paper. A feud developed with monumental results. Sensational headlines in the Rock Island News astonished citizens: "Schriver's Shame, Caught in a House of Ill Fame in Peoria with Ethel, a Prostitute that Finds Schriver Disgusting." By such tactics, Looney eventually achieved his goal; the mayor was discredited and his reputation ruined.

Before World War I, Billburg built the bar of his dreams, a tavern that was half a block long with a bar that extended the length of the building. It was called "The Longest Bar in the World" and it well could have been. Patrons came from everywhere to quench their parched throats in his beautiful bar. Even judges would stop in for a quick one before stepping to the bench. When the war began, the government closed the business, saying "The Longest Bar in the World" was too close to a military installation, the Rock Island Arsenal. Alcoholic beverages were illegal, they declared.

Billburg was devastated, but reopened his saloon as a restaurant and soft-drink parlor. The restaurant was already well-known to the public. The drinks were different. The military authorities watched him carefully — some of the time. Behind the bar, in very concealed places, Billburg and other bartenders would use ingenious methods of hiding illegal booze — behind paneling or beneath slats in the floor. Those watching knew it, but they liked a drink or two themselves — for free. The payoffs continued, even to government officials.

During Looney's self-imposed absence in New Mexico, his former lieutenants Billburg and Drost and a few city officials took over control of vice in the city. When Looney returned, he hired Emeal Davis, a huge black man, to replace Billburg as his bodyguard and enforcer. Looney also incorporated his son, Connor, into the family crime business.

By 1922, Looney's organization had been rebuilt to its largest and most powerful point ever, and his former antagonist, Mayor Harry H. Schriver, was now an ally. Looney had tentacles that reached across the nation. In anticipation of a national Grotto convention coming to town in June, Looney's collectors sold protection throughout Rock Island to law violators. At the time, within two blocks of city hall you could find 14 places where there were daily open violations of the law. Some were houses of prostitution, some gambling houses, some bootlegging places and others were a variety of combinations of them all. Within five blocks of city hall, there were 27 such places, and within nine blocks there were 39, according to The Argus.

When Prohibition agents came to Rock Island in July to follow up on raids they had made during the Grotto convention, William Gabel, who ran a saloon at 2319 4th Avenue, met with federal agent R.C. Goss. Gabel gave Goss canceled payoff checks, and the agent reportedly boasted that he had them. There were nine checks, ranging from $75 to $500, which Gabel had given to Looney henchman Louis Ortell in exchange for being allowed to do business.

* * * * *

Another chink in Looney's previously impenetrable armor was a split with Cy Hazlett after Hazlett and Connor Looney got into a fight over a woman. Telephone operator Hazel Schadel was a divorcee with a 4-year-old son who had come to Davenport from Chicago. She had been dating Hazlett. One day, the couple and Fern Ehlers went to the back bar of the Sherman Hotel for a drink. Connor Looney came into the bar in a rage and dragged Mrs. Schadel outside. Hazlett put a gun to the young Looney's ribs, and Connor drew his own revolver. Mrs. Schadel stepped between the two and ended up leaving with Looney. Hazlett then was fired from The News by John Looney and accepted a job with the federal prohibition agents who were trying to expose the Looney crime organization. Evidence he helped provide enabled them to serve a warrant on Conner Looney for bootlegging.

Meanwhile, Gabel had grown weary of turning over his profits to Looney's protection ring. It was rumored that Looney had a plan to drive him out of business and then turn his place over to another underworld character, who would be expected to fatten the receipts. Gabel had been buying liquor and protection from Looney through Ortell for $8 per gallon — later buying some from Ortell and some from Heinie Lee, who was Helen Van Dales' brother-in-law. One day, Ortell went to collect from Gabel but returned to report to Looney that Gabel wouldn't pay the assessment unless he saw proof that Helen Van Dale had paid a like amount.

When Lee, too, could get no more orders from Gabel, Looney told him to find out why. Lee reported back that $8 a gallon was too much when he could buy liquor elsewhere for $4 per gallon. Lee warned that it was better to pay more and have the protection and carry on business unmolested.

Backed into a corner, Gabel, a former policeman, went to the feds and agreed to turn over the cancelled checks, which could then be used as evidence against Looney, since he had endorsed a number of them as his part of the illegal take. Goss had already arrested a number of bootleggers, some of whom Looney represented as an attorney.

On July 31, 1922, Gabel was gunned down as he got out of his car in front of his saloon on

*The stolen Lincoln used in the murder of Bill Gabel.*

Fourth Avenue. According to later testimony, Looney's goons spent the two nights prior to the murder stalking Gabel. At one point, Connor Looney had Gabel in his sights with his gun aimed through the fence, but his father called him off. The night before the murder, Emeal Davis, "Fat" Walker, "Shorty" Burns and Joe Zeringer cleaned their guns in preparation. On that Monday night, Connor Looney and Emeal Davis left Davis' house of prostitution in a Lincoln. They picked up John Looney, who was walking along the street wearing an old sweater, dark trousers and shoes, a cap, goggles, tight little hat, sheepskin robe and a red or blue handkerchief around his neck. According to reports, they met another car whose lights were turned off and on, in some kind of signal.

They went back to Davis's whorehouse, dropped off Davis and drove to Ortell's. John Looney got into Ortell's car and they drove to Auroch's Saloon where they met Lawrence Pedigo. Ortell went inside and asked where Gabel was.

"The old man is out there, and we're going to bump off Gabel tonight," Ortell told them.

Auroch was told to get Gabel, Goss and a woman, and take them to Davenport. Once in Iowa, the plan was to have the trio arrested and searched, hoping to get back the incriminating checks. Looney said he "had it framed in Davenport for Goss and Gabel to be arrested for disorderly conduct" so that the checks could be retrieved.

Ortell went back to the car, Looney got back into the Lincoln, and Ortell drove off. The Lincoln drove around to the back of the Gabel property where it met the car that had flashed its lights. Looney sent Connor to get into the Lincoln, and he and police detective Charles "Butch" Ginnane walked down the drive between Helen Van Dale's place and Gabel's. Ginnane was known to do the bidding of Police Chief Tom Cox, who was aligned with the Looney gang.

*Police Chief
Thomas P. Cox*

Meanwhile Gabel, who had also been at Auroch's earlier that night, arrived at his business, parked his car along the curb and got out on the street side and walked around his car to the sidewalk. As he got to the rear of the car, shots rang out. Some of the shots came from the corner of the building where testimony later showed John Looney and Butch Ginnane were standing. Gabel fell to the ground dying while other bullets entered his auto.

All of the shots entered Gabel's right side. One entered his right armpit and plowed through his chest and through his heart. A second hit him in the right hip and went through his abdomen. A third hit below the hips and went into the abdomen, and a fourth struck the outside of his right calf and kneecap. A fifth shot went through his left shoulder. The bullets, all .38 caliber, were brass jacketed and lead.

Two gunmen ran back to the Lincoln and sped away to the west. The other car drove around the corner south on 24th Street and west on Fifth Avenue. A few minutes later, Connor Looney drove the Lincoln into Ortell's garage a number of blocks away. It was later learned that the men involved were the Looneys, Ginnane, Ortell, Joe "The Gadget" Richards, Tom Cox and Leonard "Fat" Walker, a notorious hit man that Davis had hired. They were driving a stolen Lincoln and Looney's Marmon roadster. Gabel's bartender, Eddie Miner, and housekeeper, Annabelle Hammis, ran outside and found Gabel bleeding profusely on the curb. The housekeeper called police just after midnight. A crowd had gathered by the time Dr. DeSilva arrived and determined Gabel was dead.

Elizabeth Thorpe, who lived at 2309 Fourth Avenue, said she saw a big, new, highly-polished car with six men (two in the front and four in the back) pass her house on Fourth Avenue. Two men leapt from the rear seat and ran up the sidewalk east toward Gabel's place. She said the shots sounded like a string of firecrackers.

The men then came back to the car and it sped down Fourth Avenue to the west. All of the men had on dark suits and wore hats and coats and she could not identify them.

Years later, Helen Cholis Forsberg, daughter of Gus Cholis, who owned Gus' Place, recalled that night. It was very hot and the windows were open. She said there were many shots and the shooting woke her up. She saw two dark cars and men shooting at Gabel. They jumped in the cars and drove off. Her father ran outside and started to head toward the victim but was confronted by Harry Fitzsimmons, a neighbor who was also a policeman.

"He was told to let it alone, go back to bed, and the cops will take care of it. So my father and neighbors went back to their homes," she recalled.

Several days later, a black automobile went through the neighborhood and told residents not to testify about what they had seen or heard. They were told "it would go hard on them if they talked about it," she said.

Pedigo, hearing about Gabel's death, phoned Connor Looney. Connor laughed and told him to go downtown and listen to comments being made about the shooting. Pedigo and Richards went to town and stopped by Gabel's place, where they saw

*The Rock Island News continued its ongoing battle with The Argus, its rival newspaper.*

his body. They called Connor and told him that Gabel was dead. He was survived by his wife, Vivian, and three brothers. He was buried at Riverside Cemetery in Marshalltown, Iowa.

Gabel's death sparked a gang war that would end in the famous Market Square gun battle. There were 12 murders in Rock Island in 1922. Three other men reportedly "committed suicide" by falling from the upper floors of downtown buildings. The Rock Island Argus led an ongoing cry of indignation that did not let up until Looney was convicted of the Gabel murder three years later, in December of 1925.

"The thing for you to keep in mind, Mr. Good Citizen, is that the murder of Bill Gabel was unwritten notice to you and the other 35,000 residents of Rock Island that the price of interference with the activities of the local underworld is death," The Argus editorialized shortly after Mr. Gabel's death. "And that threat will remain over your head just so long as you continue to tolerate the present vicious condition in your city. Rock Island belongs to you, not to the band of itinerant thugs and prostitutes."

The community was outraged. Day after day, The Argus ran a string of editorials that provoked public indignation and kept the issue from dying.

"This simply bears out what The Argus has held from the beginning — that the underworld is stronger than the city and county governments," The Argus raged on, more than a month later. "It is up to the city and county governments to prove that it isn't, and thus far they haven't proven it."

The paper also charged, "The Rock Island underworld may be somewhat unsettled as a result of its experiences of the past month, but it still retains its strangle hold on the city and county administrations, and it likely will retain it during the incumbency of the present officials."

In return, Looney's Rock Island News accused the "Dirty Argus Bunch" of being involved in the murder of Bill Gabel. "Argus Lies Nailed" read another issue of The News on September 16, 1922.

The Argus continued to demand that authorities fulfill their promises to clean up the city. Meanwhile, Looney was circulating petitions for his candidacy for county judge. He would also blame The Argus for the climax of the gang war on October 6, 1922, when the gun battle broke out on Rock Island's Market Square.

# Hell at midday

Friday, October 6, 1922, was a red-letter date in the history of organized crime in Rock Island. The largest gun battle ever waged in the streets of the city ended in the death of John Looney's son, John Connor Looney.

Argus headlines that day screamed across the paper's front page: "John Looney Jr. Probably Fatally Wounded In Market Square Gun Fight. Bystander Also Felled by Bullets Showered in Front of Sherman Hotel. Panic Caused in Rock Island Business Section by Affray Thought to Have Been Climax of an Underworld Feud."

*The Market Square gun battle and fatal shooting of Connor Looney made headlines in the October 6, 1922 Rock Island Argus.*

*The Rock Island Argus offices on Second Avenue attracted crowds of baseball fans during the World Series in the years before radio and television. Telegraphic play-by-play was posted in the windows. This group was watching the account of a game between the New York Giants and New York Yankees in 1922, when the Market Square gun battle broke out. Argus building is located in the background at right.*

The gun battle took place at two in the afternoon while hundreds of people were gathered downtown to watch the baseball scoreboard in the front window of The Argus for results of the World Series game between the New York Giants and New York Yankees.

"Scores along the street narrowly escaped the flying bullets," The Argus reported. "The revolver battle started so suddenly, went along so wildly and fiercely, that residents along the block ran for cover. They caught only fleeting glimpses of the participants, and their stories, when the conflict quieted down, were at wide variance," The Argus said.

It was raining and 88 degrees — warm for October. John Looney and his son reached the Sherman Hotel just before two o'clock. Lawrence Pedigo, an associate of the Looneys and operator of the Sherman Hotel, parked behind the Looneys' car.

Soon, two cars filled with men pulled up opposite the Looney and Pedigo cars in the middle of the street. The men stood up, pulled revolvers, and the greatest gunfight in the history of the city was on.

Pedigo and Connor Looney, then 21, were in the

*This photo from official police files of the Market Square gun battle shows a bullet hole in the front window of the Sherman Hotel.*

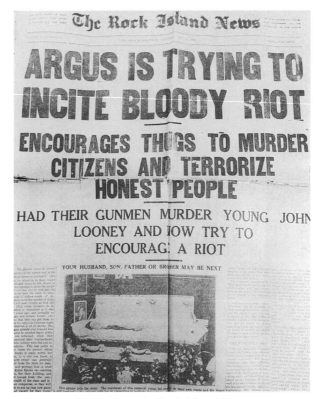

*This is how the Rock Island News reported the death of Connor Looney.*

street and started toward the hotel lobby. Connor Looney fell, hit by the first shot. He made a futile attempt to use his revolver, which apparently had jammed.

"Get upstairs and shoot it out; we got no chance here," yelled Pedigo.

*Official police file photo show the scene of the Market Square shootout in 1922.*
*At the far right is the Sherman Hotel. A police officer can been seen standing in the street,*
*just in front of the parked automobiles, at the location where Looney's car was parked.*

At this point, Albert J. Allguyer of Brooklyn, New York, who was in town looking for work, started toward the wounded Connor Looney and was shot in the stomach, while Pedigo and John Looney reached the hotel.

*John Connor Looney*

"Within a few seconds, bullets poured out of the second-floor windows of the Sherman, and the crowd, which had been attracted at the first volley of shots, swung back as lead whizzed over their heads and the bullets cracked along the pavement," said The Argus. Bullets cracked the windows of the hotel and cracked against the brick storefronts. Finally out of ammunition, the two big cars turned and tore up 3rd Avenue with police in pursuit.

The wounded Allguyer was taken to Martin's Cigar Store and stretched out on the floor near the entrance. "He bled profusely, and his clothing was soon a soggy mass of gore," The Argus reported. He told an Argus reporter he had been standing in front of The Argus, watching the

*This official police crime scene photo is a closer view of the Sherman Hotel.*
*A police officer again is standing in the location of Looney's car, just to the right*
*of the telephone pole. Looney and Lawrence Pedigo returned fire from the second*
*floor windows while Connor Looney was gunned down in the street.*
*The hotel site is a parking lot today.*

scoreboard, when he heard the first shots fired and rushed to the scene of the shooting.

"Bullets were then flying thick and fast," he said.

"Before I reached the street in front of the Sherman Hotel, a bullet struck me. I fell to the street. I guess they potted me a good one." He was later taken to St. Anthony's Hospital.

Four men were charged in the shooting. George "Crimps" Holsapple was arrested within a few minutes of the shooting, filling the radiator of his car. Also arrested were Dan Drost, former editor of The News, who had been shot in the left arm; George Buckley, a former saloon keeper; and Anthony Billburg, whom The Argus called a "former saloon man and longtime enemy of the Looney gang," even though at one time he had been a lieutenant of Looney's. A fifth person involved in the hit, Jake Ramser, was never charged.

At the coroner's inquest, John Looney began his testimony in low tones, but could scarcely be heard by the jurors and was asked to speak louder.

He testified that he was sitting in the car. They had stopped at the hotel to get some papers from Pedigo. As the two cars drove up, Looney testified, his son said, "There's Billburg."

"I saw Billburg and Jake Ramser, and it looked like Ramser was looking right at me," Looney told the coroner's inquest. "I said, 'There's Ramser, look out.' "

Looney said he took his revolver from a pocket in the door and put it in his coat. "I jumped from the car onto the sidewalk, and there I saw it all in front of me. I saw Billburg, Drost and Ramser in the cars. I then said again, 'Come, my boy, come.' "

After jumping to the sidewalk, Connor Looney came around the front of the car, Looney testified. John Looney ran for the hotel door.

"It seemed like the whole thing was over in 10 seconds. A volley of shots came, and I reached for the door. The boy fell, and I turned around and shot straight at Drost. The boy started to get up on his feet. Pedigo ran up the stairs and shot through the window. I ran to the boy, who had fallen on the sidewalk with his head facing west.

"He turned to me and said. 'They got me, they got me.'

"When I turned, I saw Billburg. I saw Ramser and Drost on the ground. They all seemed to be firing at me. I saw they had a shotgun and a rifle. They all wanted to kill me," said Looney.

"They looked as if they were all firing towards us. Drost was shooting at me and I was shooting at him. I thought that I had hit him, but I am not sure," Pedigo later told police.

When asked if he and his son had ever been threatened, Looney replied, "There hasn't been a day gone by, hardly, but what I received a threat of some kind."

The day after the shooting, The Argus reported that Connor Looney, 21, had died of his wounds. One bullet had "pierced the center of his abdomen and perforated the intestines 14 times." Another bullet fractured a bone in his leg. It was also reported that a bullet pierced the spinal column.

"A charge of more than 100 buckshot tore the flesh of his right buttock. The other bullets struck him in the arms," The Argus said.

Brother-in-law Frank Hamblin donated a pint of blood for a transfusion, but it would not save Connor's life. A chunk of his body had been torn away by the shotgun blast, and he was bleeding internally. At St. Anthony's Hospital, John Looney kept a death watch over his son, occasionally shouting violent oaths of revenge. Death came at 10:20 that night, eight hours after the shooting.

John Looney and Dr. Joseph DeSilva were at Connor Looney's bedside when he died.

No charges were filed against John Looney.

"We have several witnesses who say that he was not seen to produce a gun or fire a shot until he was upstairs in the hotel," Rock Island County Sheriff John G.

Miller said. "His shooting was in self-defense against an attempt to murder, and he can't be held for that."

Assistant States Attorney Edward L. Eagle said, "Everything we have found substantiates the theory that this was a war between two rival factions. Our evidence indicates that the men who manned the two cars from which the shooting came went out with the express purpose of killing Looney and his son, and perhaps Pedigo."

In the same October 7 issue, The Argus reported that Connor Looney had been made a special police officer, allowing him to carry a badge and a gun. The permit was approved by Mayor Harry M. Schriver. Also in that day's paper, The Argus asked again, "Who killed Bill Gabel?"

*Assistant States Attorney Edward L. Eagle*

The headlines in the next Rock Island News read: "R.I. Argus Thugs Kill John Looney Jr." A secondary headline continued: "Insinuations of Dirty Sheet Direct Cause of Murder."

A group of local businessmen led by jeweler Jake Ramser had approached Billburg about killing John Looney. He was told not to worry, that everything would be taken care of and that they would never be prosecuted. Billburg later tried to change his story and implicate some of the businessmen in the shooting of Connor Looney in testimony before a grand jury, but too many others had seen the gunmen.

In November 1924, Billburg told a grand jury that six weeks before the gun battle he was called to Ramser's Jewelry Store, where he met with Ramser, John Colligan, John Potter and Tom Haege, who suggested it was time to get rid of Looney.

"They suggested to get Looney, tie him to a tree, build a fire under him and make him confess to the killing of Bill Gabel or to torture him in some way and make him confess that he killed Bill Gabel. They even suggested to then kill Looney after

*Rock Island News charges that The Argus was responsible for the death of Connor Looney continued for several days.*

he had confessed," Billburg said. "Ramser bothered me every day. I never approved of the plans as to killing Looney."

His later account of the shooting differed greatly from that of John Looney, Pedigo and other eye witnesses. Suspicions were that he was trying to implicate those he thought were going to support him, but then didn't. On October 6, 1922, Billburg said he had just gotten out of the hospital when he got a call from Ramser.

"Come right down, I want to see you. If you want to see some excitement, get (your) friends to come down to Market Square. We are going to take Looney out and kill him."

Billburg got into his car. Buckley was with him.

"I drove past Market Square, past the Looneys, and I saw Jake Ramser, Colligan, Potter and Haege and young Looney shooting at each other. The battle was already on. I had nothing to shoot with. I was half a block away from where the boy was actually killed."

Billburg testified that he went to Ramser's later that afternoon after being questioned by Assistant States Attorney Edward Eagle.

"If that boy dies there is a murder charge against someone," said Billburg.

"I hope to God I did get the boy and am sorry I didn't kill the old man, too," Ramser reportedly replied.

*John Colligan*

Billburg testified that he and Looney were not enemies. He said he had been in bed for three years and three months due to health issues, and Looney had taken control of the community. He said there were a number of people who saw the shooting who were called before the grand jury, but were never asked about Ramser. All of the questions were about Billburg, Holsapple, Drost and Buckley.

Holsapple also testified before the grand jury in 1924. He said Ramser wanted to kill Looney because he had written up his sister, and Potter wanted him because he had written up his mother. When asked why he hadn't brought this up during the trial, Holsapple said, "These fellows had promised to help us. They were supposed to pay for all these legal expenses, and that we would never see the pen. It was supposed to be fixed that we were safe."

*Mrs. Minnie Potter, publisher of the Rock Island Argus, next to her newspaper press in the 1920s — about the time of John Looney's trial.*

Some prominent citizens had raised approximately $65,000, ostensibly to prosecute the murder. But in reality, it was to shield those of higher social standing and allow those of lesser standing to bear the brunt of the crime. Despite promises of support, it was Holsapple and Billburg who hired famed attorney Clarence Darrow to defend them. Meanwhile, the Citizen's Committee, unwilling to trust the prosecution to the states attorney, brought the state attorney general and assistants Thomas Marshall, Charles Hadley and Senator James S. Barbour to Rock Island. Marshall's efforts with the grand jury reportedly were directed mainly at securing immunity, or a failure to indict some of the persons involved in planning the attack. When a witness would attempt to introduce facts against others into the hearing, Marshall would interrupt and say that only those who had been charged were being investigated, thus making the entire grand jury investigation a farce.

Other prominent citizens who had witnessed the crime declined to appear before the grand jury. Among those named in the indictments were John W. Potter, publisher of The Argus; John M. Colligan, managing editor of The Argus; Fred Mueller, advertising manager of The Argus; Thomas Haege, clothier; J.L. Vernon, former president of the People's National Bank and the American Trust and Savings Bank; insurance agent Harry H. Cleaveland; and Walter Rosenfield, local businessman and former chairman of the Republican State Central Committee who would be mayor from 1923-26. But many more prominent citizens of the city were rumored to be involved other than those against which indictments were sought.

Despite claims to the contrary to the grand jury, stories passed down through the Billburg family still peg Anthony Billburg as the mastermind behind the hit. His great-grandchildren still have the .38 caliber gun that was returned to Mrs. Billburg by Darrow after the trial and is believed to have fired the fatal bullets at young Looney.

Fred Sinclair, who worked for Looney's newspaper and lived at his house, later testified that fifteen days after Connor Looney's death Billburg said, "I swore to kill John Looney and I killed his son. I'll kill John Looney just as sure as I killed his son."

Shortly thereafter, James "Dude" Bowen, king of the gamblers in Rock Island, dealt from the bottom of the deck and was murdered. He reportedly had fallen behind in his payments to Looney. Marcell Martinez, who sold women and dope, was shot to death as well. In the next six days, eight people were killed.

Mayor Schriver finally challenged his police to clean up the mess.

"Battles and murder and sudden death swarmed out of the vicious depths of a dope peddler's den in Rock Island last night. Two policemen were killed and one cocaine fiend slain. Rock Island has been thrown another such furor as followed the killing of Connor Looney a week ago," wrote The Democrat in Davenport, Iowa.

Three days after the shooting, on Monday, October 9, it was announced that a prosecutor from the Illinois Attorney General's Office would investigate the murder of Bill Gabel. The next day, a force of 25 government agents was in Rock Island, gathering information.

Almost as soon as his son was buried, Looney fled to his hometown of Ottawa. He made Ottawa his headquarters for a short time before moving to Denver and finally back to his ranch in New Mexico. About the same time, he was indicted by the U.S. Court in Peoria for transporting stolen autos across state lines.

Meanwhile, Pedigo produced a telegram:

"We are on the way to Rock Island."

(signed)

"The cowboys at the ranch."

"I don't know what they're coming for. You can guess," said Pedigo.

Connor had grown up with the cowboys on the ranch and they had grown to like him. There was a general fear of what would happen when they arrived. Only a few of them actually turned up for the funeral, which was held at St. Joseph's Church after Connor had laid in state for a week at the Moeller Undertaking Parlor, 2030 Fourth Avenue. Connor Looney lay in his casket, covered by a silken shroud with burning candles at head and foot.

The church was completely full for his funeral, and a crowd of curiosity seekers brought total attendance to about one thousand, filling the church, the hall and pavement outside. About 80 percent of the spectators were women, and a dozen floral pieces were used at the church and at the gravesite. Six policemen and detectives were scattered through the crowd in case there was any trouble.

The Rev. P.H. Durkin of St. Joseph's Catholic Church celebrated the Mass and the Rev. C.P. O'Neill assisted at the brief service at the cemetery. Near the beginning of the service, Ursula, who had been in St. Anthony's Hospital, fainted and was taken by her father, her aunt Mrs. J.L. O'Connor and Pedigo, back to the hospital. Looney returned later and stood at the back door of the church; Pedigo waited by the car.

At the cemetery, flowers were banked under the canvas canopy covering the burial plot. Connor was laid to rest high on a wind-swept hill in old Calvary Cemetery. There is no headstone.

# Historic legal problems

Less than three weeks after the shootout at Market Square, all of Looney's saloons and brothels were closed. Six stills, capable of making 300 gallons of bootleg booze a day, were destroyed. Looney's home was raided and its arms cache seized. The News ceased publication. John Looney was indicted for auto theft by a federal grand jury in Peoria in October of 1922, and then for the murder of William Gabel.

Except Looney was nowhere to be found.

The Red Rose Saloon, run by Emeal Davis and located at Fourth Avenue and LeClaire Street, was closed. Leonard "Fat" Walker, manager of the Red Rose, was ordered to leave town or spend 30 days in jail for messing up a police officer's uniform. Walker had hit another man with the butt of his revolver, and it took a squad of police to break up the struggle that followed.

"The Red Rose has been a place for drunken brawls, hooch and immoral lifestyle for some time," The Davenport Times reported.

Allen "Chicago Whitey" Fordney was arrested in Davenport and confessed that he was brought to Rock Island as a bodyguard for John Looney. He turned against Looney after he was shorted money promised him as part of the stolen-car ring. Stanley Kasmouski (alias Albert Wagner, alias Karl Stanley, alias Joe Kasmouski), who Fordney said was brought to town to kill Looney, was arrested in Rock Island. In all, four men imported by the gangs in Rock Island were arrested in mid-November of 1922. All were ex-cons wanted in various parts of the country. Most were part of Looney's stolen-car ring.

Many known Looney associates were arrested and fined. Elle Donahue, a madam

*Newspaper photo of Lawrence Pedigo, center, with his girlfriend Geraldine Hunter, left, and mother Sallie Bryant.*

from a Davenport house of ill repute, and Mrs. Grace Philbee, Looney's photographer, turned witnesses against him. Robert Kinner, the "Punch Board King" of the Bijou Cigar Store on Second Avenue and distributor for the mob, was also charged.

Looney's empire was crumbling.

Charges piled up. He was charged with conspiracy to murder Dan Drost, along with Louis Ortell, Gint Hippert, Lawrence Pedigo and others. He was also charged, along with Pedigo, with conspiracy to obtain money from Israel Meyer through fraud and false pretense. He and Cox were charged with larceny in the theft of an automobile valued at $300 from the city of Rock Island after Cox gave Looney a stolen car stored in the police garage. It was shipped to Looney's ranch, and Cox also provided a letter of clearance for police along the way. The indictment prompted Cox's resignation on December 5, 1922.

*George Holsapple*

In all, at least 10 indictments and a bond of at least $70,000 awaited Looney when captured.

Most importantly, in December of 1922, Looney, Cox, Pedigo, Joe "The Gadget" Richards and Walker were charged with the murder of William Gabel. Then, in January of 1923, an indictment was returned against Looney, Mayor Harry M. Schriver, City Attorney John K. Scott, Police Chief Thomas Cox, Pedigo and Robert Kinner for conspiracy to furnish punch board and other gaming devices to diverse persons and diverse keepers of houses of prostitution and also to provide "protection" while operating such gaming devices, saloons, gaming houses and houses of ill repute. Kinner was granted a severance from the case. Scott's portion was continued; he would later get off.

*George Buckley*

Cox died before he was tried. Whether it was due to the stress and strain on his family, his relationship with Van Dale, his job, image and the thought of a police chief going to prison, or whether he poisoned himself, depends on which sources you believe. Schriver and Pedigo were tried and convicted.

In September 1923, Anthony Billburg, George Holsapple, George Buckley and Dan Drost went to trial for the murder of Connor Looney. They were defended by famed attorney Clarence Darrow and Ben Stewart. Assistant attorneys general Charles Hadley and James J. Barbour handled the prosecution, along with Rock Island County States Attorney Ben S. Bell and his special assistant, George W. Wood, of Moline.

With such an assembly, those in the courtroom knew they would not only witness an historic verdict, but were also in for some great oratory.

Billburg sat calmly throughout the trial — watchful and attentive at all times. Holsapple took the case rather humorously; he smiled frequently at testimony and never seemed to be worried. Buckley was calm and self-controlled throughout. He seldom spoke when in the courtroom, but if he did it was always in smooth, quiet tones and with a smile. As the trial neared an end, his face became thinner and the lines were more drawn, but he was never outwardly nervous. Drost was uneasy and when sessions would recess for the noon hour, he would wander aimlessly about the corridors or courthouse grounds, seldom speaking to anyone.

By this time, Darrow, the famous attorney defending them, was well past his prime. He didn't pay much attention to the law. He just worked the facts. He would get up each morning, eat a hearty breakfast, and then wouldn't eat again until he had finished his work for the day, often going to midnight. He was endowed with a remarkable memory, was a quick observer and could retain information without notes.

Clearly, time had caught up with Darrow by the time he defended Billburg and the others. At an earlier trial, his wife noted his appearance had changed. His face was haggard, the muscles on his face twitched, and the lines around his eyes and mouth told of worry and sleepless nights. Darrow had become very thin and began to drink. A woman sitting at the table with him at dinner one night said he was one of the dirtiest men she had ever seen.

During his closing arguments, Darrow was calm and calculating, his nerves never wavered. He was a tiger at the bar as he made his argument. He was a spirited orator and played the part of the grand old man. He looked directly into the eyes of each juror and, with a calming effect, went directly to the heart of the case. His case was one of psychology and humanity.

But the prosecutors were confident and went on the offensive.

"Billburg's hands were red, dripping with blood, but they weren't satisfied. They wanted more blood, and even after the Market Square battle these defendants concocted a scheme against Looney," said Hadley in his September 14 closing arguments.

He paused and walked toward the jury.

"This was a fight not to rid the community of Looney, but to place Billburg back on the throne in that room, so that he could say, 'Come here. You pay $200 a month, and you pay $150, and you and you and you. That's the reason for the battle in Market Square that day. This was a battle that the underworld must again bow to King Billburg in his lust for the dirty money, the filthy lucre.

"This was an attempt by a vice lord and his associates to kill the man who stood in his way, but instead they killed a boy. A young man who sought to protect his father, and instead of coming here to say they killed this boy, they try to give you the impression that he was a very bad person," Hadley continued.

Darrow ran his fingers through his hair, looked slowly toward the jury and returned the volley in his closing remarks for the defense. Other than the occasional wave of murmuring, you could hear a pin drop.

"Here are four men before you charged with killing John Connor Looney. I shall attempt to bring no tears as my friend, (prosecutor) Barbour did. There is no sorrow for John Connor Looney to be considered in this case. It is the facts that count, not the emotions. The question is, are they guilty or not guilty? I think without a reasonable doubt that they are innocent," said Darrow.

"No doubt some were honest, and again, no doubt some were not. But this case is built on the testimony of Pedigo, Ortell, Sinclair and Spangler. Who are they? And I'll add Dan Drost to those names. Men who collaborated and worked with John Looney for years. Why you would probably run if you knew these men were in an alley that you had to go through? Yet, they testify and on their statements the state will ask … I don't know what they will ask, and I don't care," Darrow said, gesturing aimlessly into the air.

"They base it all on this conspiracy, meaning that two or more men got together to come to an agreement to do an unlawful act. There is no evidence to show there was a conspiracy in existence. There was no intent. It is true they had guns when they drove up to Market Square. Then, the fact that the two men were in cars together is a circumstance. It might mean anything. There are plenty of reasons why they might have been together. Crime was the last incentive to be considered.

"Now let's go further into the wonderful conspiracy that these men have spit out of their own brains as a spider weaves his web to catch wary flies, and then to try to show a motive. They say Billburg hated him. Who swears to that? Pedigo, Ortell, Sinclair, anyone else? Not one.

"What of Pedigo? Will you tell me why a man is under so many indictments in courts that he can't count them? Will you tell me why he has met and conferred with the detectives in this case, and the state's attorneys? There is just one answer — that he is thinking of himself and clemency for him. He is practically led into this court room by a halter. He is the associate and friend of John Looney, whose blood-red hands hang over this case, as for years they have hung like a shadow over this town," Darrow said in closing.

But Hadley was not yet done.

"King Billburg, controller of vice. The man that needs no monument to his memory. Rock Island will remember him forever. The man from who babes in the cradle will cringe. The man who people will hiss at on the streets," Hadley said in his closing rebuttal, facing Billburg. His eyes flashed fearlessly.

"Damn the witnesses of the state if you will," he said in answer to Darrow. "They were Billburg's pals. In damning our witnesses, you damn him. They were his associates, and that is the worst thing I know of them." He branded the shootout as an example of anarchy, "breaking the laws of justice until the square ran red with the blood of their endeavors."

Then he recited the details of the automobiles traveling from the Long Bar on 20th Street to Market Square.

"This meeting was planned. It was not a chance happening. And there is no doubt about the law in this case. There is no doubt about the happening. These men got together with a common purpose — to kill the Looneys. That's why these two cars came down those streets and swung into Market Square. … The defense has failed to explain their presence there. They were not hunting rabbits in Market Square at 2 o'clock in the afternoon, with rifles, pistols and shotguns," he said.

Then Hadley turned to the jury.

"You swore before the trial that you would be governed by the facts of this case, and not prejudiced by any hatred you might have for John Looney and his paper. And it is on the evidence given in this case, on the indictment of these four men that you must deliberate, according to your oath."

With that, the twelve-and-a-half day trial came to an end. On that day, in that courtroom, the famous defender and his team were bested by the state. Darrow lost. Billburg was convicted of murder and sentenced to 20 years in prison in Joliet. Holsapple, Buckley and Drost each got 14 years in the pen. An appeal was filed, but denied in December 1924.

Meanwhile, with her father on the lam, Ursula Hamblin returned to Rock Island in February 1923 to try and prevent the sale of the Looney farm on the Rock River. In a mortgage foreclosure proceeding, the findings of master-in-chancery James F. Murphy were upheld by the court and the 60-acre farm was ordered sold. Mrs. Hamblin unsuccessfully appealed the ruling to the Appellate Court.

When Ursula had returned to Rock Island two months earlier, she had filed a deed by which on December 18 in Denver John Looney had transferred the land to her. She sought a delay before the master-in-chancery by claiming Looney was ill and unable to appear. But no information was given as to where he was being treated and there was no doctor's certificate, so it was ruled that there was nothing on which to act. The hearings progressed and findings were returned to the Circuit Court in favor of the Arp estate, which held the mortgage on the land. The Arps were granted a $19,000 debt claim against Looney and the land was sold.

The Argus reported in August 1923 that Looney had established his new headquarters in Ottawa and that it was common knowledge in that community. In January of that year, police had found a Lincoln, stolen from Harry Stromberg, an illegal booze operator in Davenport, half-buried under corn in a crib near the Charles and John Ulrich farms three miles north of Ottawa. Frank and Ursula Hamblin were visiting the farm at the time. It took two visits for officers to get the auto, believed to have been used in the murder of Bill Gabel. The car had been seen in Looney's possession prior to the murder, but disappeared after the shooting.

" 'They don't want Looney very bad in Rock Island or they would come here and get him,' you hear on every tongue," The Argus reported of Ottawa residents. Looney henchmen also had been seen in Ottawa. It was generally known that Looney and his daughter, Ursula, were living on the Charles Ulrich farm in Dayton

Township. Mrs. Ulrich and Mr. Looney's late wife, Nora, had been close friends, having worked together at the millinery shop.

"Looney has 30 relatives in Ottawa. And he has some close friends who aren't a bit interested in seeing him bound for Rock Island. Ottawa is a city of 12,000 people. Everybody knows everyone else. Go to Ottawa, and you're immediately stamped a stranger," The Argus explained.

The seclusion of the Ulrich Farm made it an ideal hiding place. If Looney got a tip, he could be miles away from the farm before officers got there. A cousin, Jerry Looney, was a desk sergeant at the police station, and Looney also had close friends in the sheriff's department. Sheriff E.J. Welton told an Argus reporter that he had made two trips to the Ulrich Farm but found no trace of Looney. Another story told around town was that federal officers visited the farm in the spring of 1923 and actually talked with Looney, but didn't know it was him because he was in disguise and posing as a handyman working at the farm.

"People here think he isn't wanted in Rock Island or he would have been picked up long ago," one man told The Argus.

"Looney's capture means more to Rock Island than to Ottawa. People laugh and think it's a joke. Looney is an interesting character to them. Why wouldn't he be? He's the only native son of Ottawa who has gone out across the state, created a riot that brought militia to a city and, 10 years later, while active in the very same city, made the streamers in newspapers in practically every city in the nation, creating front-page reading matter for weeks at a time. No other Ottawan has done this," The Argus said, letting its anti-Looney prejudice show just a bit.

The paper also reported that Looney's Ottawa attorney, J.J. Conway, had said that Looney was not afraid of the law and believed that public opinion against him would wane so that some day he could return safely to Rock Island. But John Looney eventually abandoned even Ottawa, going first to Denver and then New Mexico.

In New Mexico, Looney didn't even stop long enough to gather up his cattle or horses. He did pick up his race horses, which were well cared for in a special stable, and his three gunslingers named Ward, Faulk and Steel, and headed south to Mexico. Bob Hainie from Española would show up later to gather Looney's horses, which he had bought. Looney was on the run in Mexico and elsewhere for several years.

# In the jail house now

Folks in New Mexico paid little attention to John Looney, as had generally been the case for years. They either didn't care what he was up to or were afraid to get involved with him. His ranch seemed a sanctuary — safe from everyone.

In February 1924, a $2,000 reward was offered for Looney's capture. "Wanted" posters were distributed throughout the country. The offer raised some eyebrows, but not enough for anyone to rat him out — that is, until a fateful day in November.

L.C. Oliver was a tall, gaunt man, slightly deaf, with a long mustache. Because of his deafness, he made a hobby of studying people's faces. He had served as a deputy sheriff and a town officer at various times, but now was just running his ranch near Belen, New Mexico. He had been attracted to the "wanted" posters for John Looney because of the reward they offered.

Oliver had come to town on business just before Thanksgiving. He walked up the main street of Belen and casually glanced in the window of the hotel. His gaze caught a man sitting in the lobby. He was a stranger in Belen, and strangers in small towns did not escape notice.

Oliver went to the post office where he

87

studied the "wanted" poster, with pictures of Looney both clean-shaved and with a beard. While the man he had seen had a mustache, he was sure it was Looney.

"I felt sure that I could not be mistaken. There were certain features that were so unmistakable that I was struck with the thought that it was Looney as soon as I happened to glance at him in passing the hotel," Oliver said. "I wanted to be sure and so returned to the post office to look at his pictures, but I would not have done so had I had any idea that he suspected he was being watched or had I thought there was any danger of him getting away in the meantime. I knew it was Looney, and my second study of the pictures only confirmed my belief."

He made a second trip to the hotel and was convinced. Oliver sought out the postmaster and shared his suspicions. The postmaster referred Oliver to the mayor and the deputy sheriff, who went with Oliver to the hotel where he pointed out Looney.

Looney was in the dining room. When he had finished his meal, he was greeted by officers who quietly instructed him to follow them into a back room, where the mayor and marshal made the arrest.

When confronted, Looney was indignant. They searched him. No gun. It was a crime to carry a gun, and not carrying one was part of Looney's scheme to avoid excuses for detention. Department of Justice officials in Albuquerque were notified. When the sheriff arrived, the prisoner was turned over to be held on the federal charge of transporting a stolen automobile from Muscatine, Iowa, to Rock Island, Illinois, in violation of the Dyer Act.

*John Looney*

It was over.

Those who knew Looney well said he had a strong belief in omens of good and back luck. His luck had finally run out.

It was later speculated that Looney came to Belen that day to receive cash he desperately needed to finance his continued flight from authorities. Just as he had so many times before, Looney did his best to bluff his way out of trouble using the alias Frank Hartman — complete with appropriate credentials and identification.

"I'm Frank Hartman," Looney protested. "See here's my watch with my initials F.H. and here's my Elk Lodge charm" with initials and inscription of a California lodge.

"I am a poor man and you are making a mistake. I do not know John Looney but if you hold me for him, it will be a false arrest. You can't detain me. I am a sick man and on my way home."

It didn't work, and he was arrested. A wire to the Elk Lodge in California revealed no Hartman with those initials among its members. Looney then faced United States District Attorney George R. Craig.

"You're Looney, all right," said Craig. "I met you eight years ago. Your mustache can't fool me."

Looney gave up and admitted that the name he had given, Hartman, was an alias and that he was John Looney.

On Friday, November 30, Craig had the prisoner removed to the federal section of the state penitentiary at Santa Fe, pending appearance in federal court in the New Mexico state capitol the following Monday. Looney was taken to Santa Fe by auto with his daughter, Ursula, and her husband, Frank Hamblin, following in their car.

Looney told his daughter that he had not been feeling well. Persons who had known him said he had aged greatly in the last year or two. Because of Looney's illness, the hearing was changed to Tuesday. At that hearing, Rock Island County Sheriff Clarence E. Edwards presented seven different indictments.

"I am here to take John Looney back to Rock Island, Illinois, and there are indictments in my hand. It is my duty under the law to protect John Looney with my life, if necessary. He should go back to stand trial for various charges, including murder," the sheriff said.

"I'll bet a nickel before these officers that my federal case will be dismissed without ever coming to trial. It will be dismissed by the district attorney at Peoria," Looney said. He refused to agree to the extradition and promised a fight to the end.

"I am not ready to go back to Rock Island, Illinois, just now. I do not believe I could get a square deal in the Illinois courts for one thing. For I have attacked judges in my newspaper and I have attacked them justly in my opinion. And I have attacked certain banks and bankers for what I believed was their attempt to dodge just taxes. And I have also attacked the pernicious ring of officials who have looted the public treasury."

His voice rang out clear as a bell at the hearing, held in a room near the entrance to the prison hospital.

Looney told the court that there had been six assassination attempts on him in Rock Island as a result of his published attacks, and that his enemies had gone so far as to blow up his printing press with dynamite. He said that shots had been

*John Looney, indicated by the arrow, is shown leaving the federal building in Santa Fe, New Mexico, in this Rock Island Argus photo. He was chained to the left arm of Deputy Henry Seiffert. To the far right is United States Marshal Romero and to the rear are Looney's daughter, Ursula, and her husband Frank Hamblin.*

fired into his body, he had been beaten with blackjacks on the head, jaw and nose, and that a fund of $30,000 had been raised by his enemies "to get John Looney."

"I have made enemies, many of them among the so-called moneyed classes in Rock Island, and I shall continue the fight unless my enemies kill me as they have tried to do again and again," said Looney.

He argued that he was not a fugitive but a citizen of New Mexico, having had the ranch in Rio Arriba County for more than a decade. He said he had been away from the ranch recently visiting the "hot springs." When arrested, he wore no disguise and was unarmed. He said he had traveled around New Mexico quite a bit.

At the end of the hearing, Looney was granted a continuance until December 15 to fight his extradition and substantiate reports of illness. Rock Island officials present said Looney looked to be in as good health as 20 years earlier and appeared to have put on a few pounds. Governor James F. Hinkle of New Mexico said he would not sign extradition papers on the state murder charges until after the federal charge of transporting stolen automobiles had been resolved.

However, on December 4, after receiving papers from Illinois Governor Len Small requesting extradition, Governor Hinkle said he would not hesitate to approve extradition once he had approval from Attorney General J.M. Armstrong of New Mexico as to the legality of the Illinois request.

"Mr. Looney is an interesting character," wrote a reporter for the Santa Fe New Mexican newspaper. "A man past 50 years of age, he has coal black hair which is turning grey at the ends. He has a black mustache which is clipped short, tooth brush type. He is a man about five feet ten inches or eleven inches in height, and his face is wrinkled and his complexion is the sallow one of a sick man. He has large, piercing eyes. His nose shows by its breadth and irregular line that it has been broken.

"Lawyer, newspaper publisher and politician, Looney has been a fighter," the reporter wrote. "He has been close to death on a half dozen occasions, according to detailed statements he made. And it is pretty well established that his son, John Looney Jr., brought up on a New Mexico ranch, was killed last year before Looney's eyes.

"Looney is said to be broken in health, and broken in finances, but enemy or friend would probably call him today a striking type of a game fighter."

One New Mexico rancher told the newspaper that he had known Looney since he came to New Mexico and that his ranch was probably worth $400,000. It was rumored that Looney had assets of about $1 million, but whether he had much cash at the time was a matter of speculation, and might have led to his capture.

The federal indictment against Looney for auto theft had been issued in October 1922 and contained three counts — theft of an automobile, interstate transportation of an automobile and possession of a stolen car. The federal grand jury took over after a Rock Island grand jury was unable to obtain evidence. The feds forced a confession from a man who refused to testify before the local grand jury.

The car in the case, valued at $1,000, was stolen from Charles Dyche's garage in Muscatine, Iowa, on August 29, 1922. On October 17, it was found in Henry McCarthy's barn near the Rock River in Rock Island. The car had been repainted, the engine number altered and numerous identifying accessories removed. The thieves had neglected to remove the car's serial number and a dent, from which Mr. Dyche was able to identify it.

McCarthy told Sheriff John Miller and officers Dennis Bennett and Earl Shannon that John Looney and his son had brought the car to him for storage. After telling his story to the police, he was taken before the grand jury in Rock Island, where he told the jurors that William Allen, a Looney attorney, had told him to keep quiet.

William R. Schroeder, assistant federal district attorney in Peoria, then called in McCarthy, his son Joseph, Sheriff Miller, and a policeman and a newspaperman to whom McCarthy had talked. McCarthy agreed to testify and the indictments followed.

"I wouldn't talk before because Allen told me Looney said I should keep my mouth shut," he said.

Looney was held in Santa Fe for some time before finally furnishing bail. He then came to Peoria under a murder bond, but Illinois refused to accept the New Mexico bond, and he was jailed again. His travels eventually brought him full circle — back to Rock Island to face trial after appearing in federal court in Peoria December 1 to answer to the auto theft charges.

On December 27, 1924, John Looney arrived back in Rock Island and was confined to the Rock Island County Jail. He was suffering from a bad cold and complained about the other 10 inmates who were smoking tobacco day and night. He said he could not take the fumes and was continually coughing up phlegm and blood. Other prisoners complained that they could not sleep due to Looney's coughing, and he was removed to the hospital ward.

Looney was kept in jail under various bails: $3,000 for the federal conspiracy indictment; $20,000 for the murder of Bill Gabel; $5,000 for the charge of receiving stolen property; $1,000 for an indictment of running a disorderly house; $3,000 for his indictment of running a con game; and $2,500 for conspiracy — a total of at least $34,000.

Allen, Looney's attorney, argued that the bonds were excessive and that his client's physician was concerned he would die if he remained in jail. Records show he remained in bed and ate little from January 23 to 27, 1925, and was "rapidly losing flesh and growing weaker. He suffers continually from pains in his chest and bronchitis and breathes with difficulty."

But even poor health could not help John Looney escape prosecution.

# A tightening noose

**W**hen it came time to prosecute Looney in 1925, the state attorney general said there wasn't money enough to do it, so local residents and businessmen raised $75,000. The trial was moved from the courts of Judges W.T. Church and C.J. Searle to the courtroom of Judge Nels A. Larson from Moline. Over a period of five weeks and 30 days of testimony, a seemingly endless parade of witnesses came through the courtroom to testify as to how the Looney crime organization functioned.

*Lawrence Pedigo*

Lawrence Pedigo, a former top associate, was the star witness for the state. One by one, almost without exception, Looney's crime partners and those who had benefited the most by their association with the crime boss, would roll over and testify against him.

Joe "The Gadget" Richards told the court that Connor Looney told him, "We have to get rid of a man who has squealed," but Richards told the court he had nothing to do with the shooting. He said that John Looney told him, "If anybody ever asks you if you know who killed Bill Gabel, you're always to answer, 'No.' "

Pedigo told the court, according to Argus accounts, "how the scheme of tribute and official protection made possible the operation of numerous houses of prostitution, gambling and other resorts; how Looney directed illicit business in his three hotels; how slot machines and punch-board gambling were established and protected and the profits divided; how Thomas Cox, chief of police, shared in the division of the spoils; and finally explaining how he had played his part in the lawless business without receiving more than meager compensation."

Pedigo, who testified he had been Looney's right-hand man, told the court "at one time, Tom Cox, chief of police, told Looney to 'take the whole damn police force and do what you want with it.' "

Perhaps Helen Van Dale, 32, who ran Looney's prostitution operation and was tagged Queen of the Looney Underworld, best summed up the feelings of those former criminals who testified against him when she was questioned at one of his trials.

"Mrs. Van Dale, you don't like John Looney, do you?" the prosecution asked.

"I neither like, nor dislike him. I have no reason to," she responded.

"But you are testifying against him."

"Well, I just don't know how to answer that. After he blackmailed and bled so many people, I think he should have a little justice handed him. If I told all I know about him, I could hang him," she added.

"You'd like to hang him?" the prosecutor responded.

"No."

All heads turned as she walked to the stand.

*Helen Van Dale*

The women whispered and pulled their jackets tightly closed; men, who had come to court dressed in suits, acted like little boys and pointed and elbowed each other. Helen's lengthy testimony detailed her intimate affair with police chief Cox and the illegal schemes in which he and his police aided Looney. She admitted to running a house of prostitution in Rock Island and related how she and her brother-in-law, Heinie Lee (aka Victor Cielseski), got involved in Looney's liquor trade through Cox. She said she kept books, but that her sister "Dimples" Cielseski destroyed them when Helen was arrested in December of 1922. She testified that the take was divided between herself, Cox and Looney.

The control this attractive, seductive, yet smart woman had over the chief of police was so strong that she was feared by both Cox and Looney.

On cross-examination, prosecutors asked her if she wasn't the "real" chief of police?

"When Looney didn't prevent me, yes," she answered.

While she functioned within his organization, and benefited from it, Helen Van Dale did not trust Looney. Once, she testified, she caught wind of plans by the gangster/newspaper editor to write up a male friend in The News.

"I said, if Looney ever wrote me up and said about me what he had said about other people, I would kill him and kill myself, too," said Van Dale.

"What did Looney say?" she was asked.

"He said he couldn't be killed, that the devil protected him. He told me to turn out the lights and stand over by the switch, and if his shoes were not wet, he'd light up the room," said Van Dale.

Under tough cross-examination, Van Dale admitted she had been a prostitute prior to running her own houses of prostitution and providing girls for others with Looney. She defended her sister, "Dimples," who lived with her, saying she was a housekeeper and not a prostitute.

She also testified to hearing Connor Looney say, "If Gabel squawks, I'd kill him like a dog."

In his three-and-one-half hour closing argument for Looney's first trial, Assistant Attorney General Charles W. Hadley challenged the jurors.

"We have been at this trial for 30 days. We have built up a case which shows clearly how vice in Rock Island was under the control of the Rock Island News.

"Will you be able to say to your sons and daughters that 'I have helped make the streets of Rock Island safe for my children, my wife and myself?' Will you be able to state that the thoroughfares of Rock Island are now safe to all, by your meting out punishment to this man and freeing the community from the scourge brought by this man on this city?" Hadley asked in conclusion.

At 9 a.m. on Friday, July 31, 1925, the jury returned a verdict of guilty against John Looney on charges of conspiracy to protect gambling, prostitution and illicit liquor traffic in Rock Island. Looney was calm, his right hand clenching around the left. There was a slight tightening of the mouth. No movement of the body. No flutter of an eyelash. John Looney had been prepared. In back of him, his daughter laughed to someone beside her. Then her head was buried in the curve of her arm on the bench. Shortly it was lifted. The mouth was set, but the eyes were dry. She, too, had expected what had come.

The quiet was broken by the judge's words to the jury.

The attorneys, three of them, were silent. Then the eyes of the two on one side seemed to gleam with the light of success. Across the table strewn with statute books, the eyes of the other were dim. A hand was at his mouth and the face was worn with long nervous tension.

Looney retired to an anteroom with his daughter and lawyer. Beyond the court room, the buzz of voices could be heard. Words slowly formed in Looney's mouth.

"It's a long way between here and the pen. I propose to get justice. I will motion for a new trial to prove my innocence. I intend to make my home in Rock Island County and will prove to the people that I am not guilty of the charges brought against me. I will make my home here unless I am killed or otherwise prevented from doing so."

The jury fixed the penalty at one to five years in the state penitentiary — the maximum allowed by law. Judge Larson added another 60 days in jail for contempt of court because Looney had carried a gun to the trial and called Hadley a liar. But

Looney was still fighting. While accounts said that he attempted to draw a gun while tussling with a bailiff at the beginning of his trial, he argued otherwise.

"I have a permit to carry a gun, your honor. I did not know that the statutes had been changed and only carried the gun a few days over the legal limit. I don't know who said that I tried to draw the gun, but I never even thought that I had a revolver. Drawing a gun in a courtroom would be the last thing that I would think of doing. When you say John Looney pulled a gun on a defenseless man, it is not so."

Looney did admit to calling Hadley a liar, after he had asserted that Looney's late son, Connor, was part of the conspiracy. But Looney's argument was to no avail. The noose of justice was finally beginning to tighten around John Looney.

Allen said he would seek a new trial and appeal the ruling to the Illinois Supreme Court for a writ of error. He claimed the judge had erred in admitting evidence taken from Looney's home without search warrants. But the drama was far from over, as the trial of John Looney for the murder of Bill Gabel was to quickly follow.

On that day, The Argus reprinted an editorial written October 27, 1922. It concluded: "With his son gone, Looney is deserted save by those underworld thugs he is paying to shield him in his roost under the hill. He is friendless, as he deserves to be."

\* \* \* \* \*

Looney's second trial was for the murder of Bill Gabel. It was moved to Galesburg after Looney asked for a change of venue. Judge Willis Graham of Monmouth presided. The trial began Monday, November 23, 1925, an unusually warm day, amid throngs of spectators and a circus of media coverage drawing reporters from across the country.

Escorted by deputies, Looney shuffled into the court room with a great deal of grimacing, leaning heavily on a cane and sporting a new John Barrymore-style haircut. With effort, he settled into a chair at the defendant's table and bowed politely to the prosecution. The prosecutors ignored his theatrics with the exception of Ben Bell, a Rock Island attorney who was Looney's chief antagonist for years. Bell shook his head in disbelief. Only Looney would display such an

*Judge Willis Graham*

embarrassing entrance. The prosecution had only one thing in mind — convict the criminal. They intended to destroy the man who had sneered at the law and bled the public for so long.

Looney remained in control of the defendant's table as he organized papers and whispered to his attorneys. If you hadn't known better, you would think he was the lead attorney for the defendant.

*John Looney*

He turned several times to speak to his daughter, who was seated behind him.

Eleven deputies were scattered around the room to protect the prisoner and the jury. Judge Graham presided at the south end of the court room and was flanked on the right by the circuit clerk and the left by the court reporter. The defense table, where Looney and his attorneys were seated, was directly facing the judge. Several feet away were the prosecutors. Along the south wall of the court room was the jury box. On-lookers sat on the north end of the room under the overhang of a balcony that contained several hundred chairs and could seat as many as the main floor.

The first motion by the defense was to suppress evidence used in the previous trial in Rock Island. The judge ruled against the motion. The defense argued that Looney's house had been illegally ransacked and documents seized, as well as guns and hand grenades. That motion was denied, but it was later agreed that individual rulings would be made on specific pieces of evidence instead of one blanket ruling.

Jury selection followed and the first pool was exhausted with only seven jurors picked, so court was adjourned. A second group was later exhausted. The group was fed a big Thanksgiving dinner and enjoyed a movie at the hotel. By Friday, November 27, Judge Graham erupted in anger at the jurors over the reasons being given not to serve.

Looney was visibly bored by the selection process. He stared hard at the polished hardwood floor, his mind in another place and time.

Senator James J. Barbour of Chicago, the lead attorney for the prosecution, argued that the case had received so much publicity that residents must have heard about it and formed an opinion, but he thought that was not a deterrent to being a juror.

The judge disagreed.

"I have thought this matter over carefully, and I think that a man ought not to be accepted under oath that has an opinion. A man cannot say to the attorneys on one side that he has a fixed opinion and then, although he turns around and says he can lay that opinion aside, consider the issues impartially as a fair juror," said Judge Graham.

Finally, by Monday, November 30, the jurors had been selected. Charles Hadley started his opening statement at 2:30 in the afternoon and outlined the case against Looney. He said evidence would show that Looney was involved in organizing the murder of Bill Gabel, and was present when it occurred. He then detailed the events of the night.

"The evidence will show that Ortell, preparing to retire in his home a number of blocks away, heard the shots and in a few minutes saw Connor Looney drive the Lincoln into his garage," he said, concluding his opening remarks.

In his opening statement, Looney's attorney, General O.O. Askren of Roswell, New Mexico, said that Looney was not involved in the operation of his newspaper, The News, after 1912. At that time, Looney's health became impaired and he was threatened with tuberculosis so he moved to his ranch in New Mexico, returning to Rock Island only on a few occasions to attend to business. In 1921, Looney came back from New Mexico and spent time in Rock Island and Ottawa.

"On the night of 31 July, 1922, when Gabel was shot, Looney was not there or in the vicinity, had no connection with the crime and did not even hear of it until later when the town of Rock Island was generally notified," said Askren.

"The prosecution will tell you that evidence will prove that Looney fled following the crime. I will tell you that evidence will prove that Looney stayed in Rock Island until 15 or 16 October after the shooting except on one occasion when he made a hurried trip to and from his ranch in New Mexico."

Askren said that Looney did leave after the death of his son, Connor. Looney's daughter, Ursula Hamblin, was in the hospital having given birth to a child six days before. The knowledge that her brother had been murdered caused her condition to become worse and it became necessary for Mrs. Hamblin to be taken west. Her father took her from Rock Island to Denver, Colorado, where she was placed in a hospital. Furthermore, John Looney went west because he had a mortal fear of injury from those who had fired on him and killed his son, Askren said.

More importantly, Askren pointed out to the court and history, the case against Looney was built around the word of underworld low-lifes who had been granted immunity by the prosecution.

"We do not know as to the conversations of dead men which may be introduced. We do know, however, that there will be evidence of a conspiracy to testify falsely against John Looney. Various witnesses for the state have been induced to testify because they have been promised immunity. (Emeal) Davis has been kept isolated in jail and has been promised immunity. Helen Van Dale, queen of the prostitutes, was promised immunity. She was taken from jail and promised immunity. There is no imputation against counsel for the prosecution, for I believe that they are honorable men, but I believe that they have witnesses who are disreputable and whose testimony should not be credited.

"The evidence will tend to show that John Looney tried to suppress vice instead of promote it. The evidence will not disclose the identity of the slayer by the testimony of any creditable witness, and the evidence as a whole will show that Looney was not connected with the killing," Askren said in closing.

Besides Askren, Looney was represented by R.D. Robinson of Galesburg, I.R. Wasson and John Dougherty of Peoria, and William C. Allen. The prosecution was led by State Attorney General Oscar E. Carlstrom, along with States Attorney Ben S. Bell and Edward L. Eagle of Rock Island, Charles W. Hadley of Wheaton, Robert C. Rice and S.M. Meadows of Galesburg, and the lead prosecutor, Senator James J. Barbour of Chicago.

Details of the murder were outlined. There were no eyewitnesses, so the case was built around circumstantial evidence.

On December 1, Joe "The Gadget" Richards, former proprietor of the Rex Hotel, testified that Connor Looney had told him of plans to get rid of a man. Lawrence Pedigo then testified about Looney's operations, as he had in the earlier trial. He was asked about a phone conversation with Connor Looney. Pedigo stated that when he informed Connor that Bill Gabel had been shot, Connor laughed and told him to go downtown and listen to the remarks about the shooting.

The next day, Pedigo went to the Looney home, where he found Connor and Davis with Looney. He said Looney took him to the bedroom and asked him what he had heard about the shooting.

"Everyone in town is accusing me of killing Gabel," he told Looney.

"That is what we want done," Looney replied, asking where he had been the night before. He responded that he had been with Richards and a policeman named Miner.

"That's fine," said Looney.

"Suppose they accuse you?" Pedigo asked Looney.

"Never mind that my boy, never mind," he replied.

On December 2, Hadley described what happened the night of the murder, as well as other incidents that contributed to the theory that Looney was engaged in a conspiracy to murder Gabel.

In testimony on Thursday, December 3, Pedigo also told the court that another murder was attempted by the Looney gang the day before Bill Gabel was killed. Pedigo said he was careful to set up an alibi on the night of the Gabel murder "because Davis told me that they tried to kill another man the day before that."

Over the next few days, the parade of testimony continued. Police officers and other witnesses provided bits and pieces of evidence regarding what they saw or heard on the night of the murder.

Max D. Rosenfeld, a real estate and insurance man from Moline, said he had known Looney for about 30 years. From 1917 to 1922, he had been half-owner and secretary of Abrahams Candy Company in Moline, which was where Looney and his son, Connor, got their candy and punch boards.

Louie Ortell told the court on December 8 that he had been "collecting" for Looney since 1919. The bars paid protection to Looney and Cox to sell liquor and have gambling and women. Ortell had also sold stock in the Rock Island News for Looney. He went to madams Hattie Swanson, Jennie Mills and Nell Hill and sold stock in The News in exchange for cash. Swanson paid $1,000 and Mills had to mortgage her property to take $500 in stock, he testified. He also made arrangements with the near beer places for protection "so they could run wide open during the Grotto Convention of 1922. Each of the bootleg bars was marked down for a payment of a certain size — from $250 to $1,000."

Looney wanted $1,000 from Gabel for the four-day convention, but Gabel argued he would only get two days of business, since the first and the last day people would be arriving and leaving. Ortell said they compromised at $300, but Looney wasn't satisfied and called Gabel up and they argued over the phone. Looney said Gabel would either pay the whole thousand or be closed up.

Ortell also testified that five minutes after hearing shots the night of the murder, Connor Looney drove up and pulled into his garage. "He was driving swiftly. When I went down to see what was going on, young Looney was excited and in a great hurry and refused to stop and talk. I went out and looked at the car. It had burlap sacks all around it — over the doors where one might put his hands, on the steering wheel and elsewhere. The license plates were off and the windshield was down.

"Looney came up the next day and asked me to come down to The News plant 'to see who are the enemies of Gabel.' He was awfully nervous, I would say. He tried to pick his teeth with a toothpick and couldn't hit them right," Ortell testified.

Illness to a juror, Clarence Jones from near Galva, forced a break in the testimony. Action resumed with the juror back in the jury box after a minor digestive ailment sent him to the hospital for 36 hours.

A bar owner, Henry Aurochs, testified that he was told by Ortell, "The old man is going to knock off Gabel tonight." Less than two hours later he heard Gabel was dead.

Davis, who had worked for Looney, testified that he had seen John and Connor Looney near Gabel's bar with some other unidentified men on the night of the murder.

Helen Van Dale, queen of the Looney underworld, told of discussions between the Looneys and Cox where Connor spoke of "what Gabel was going to get."

She was questioned by J.E. Daugherty and the atmosphere was tense. Helen stepped to the witness stand dressed in a mink cape, a black hat, black satin dress with a lace collar, tan shoes and stockings with tan gloves. She gave her age as 32.

Her testimony substantiated much of the other testimony involving Tom Cox and Butch Ginnane, both of whom she said she was with at the time of the murder, as well as several others who were partying with her, her sister, and two other girls in her house.

In all, the prosecution called 57 witnesses. About half were accomplices or directly linked to the criminal conspiracy that led to the Gabel murder.

To counter, the defense bolstered its argument that Looney was mostly absent from Rock Island after 1912 by introducing checks, letters, telegrams, bills of lading, passports and other papers that located him all over the west between September 1919 and June 15, 1922. Also introduced through his own testimony and that of Mr. and Mrs. Charles Ulrich was the argument that he was not in Rock Island on July 29 and 30, 1922, but in Aurora about 100 miles away, at the home of Mrs. Ulrich's father. But that testimony conflicted with that of other witnesses. Few had much to say in Looney's defense, yet he continued to deny all the charges against him.

Senator Barbour concluded with one of the most dramatic scenes in the history of Knox County Circuit Court, The Argus reported. "Put Looney in prison for life where he will no longer be a menace to society," the senator urged. On his completion, men and women in the courtroom wept and some had to leave, The Argus said.

"Bill Gabel's murder was highly effective, considering its motive," the senator said, "because it struck terror to the heart of every man, woman and child in Rock Island and, especially the satellites of John Looney."

# The dance goes on

*James J. Barbour*

**W**ith testimony complete and the year 1925 coming to a close, the anticipation heightened as the world waited to see if John Looney would be found guilty, and, if so, what his penalty would be.

In his closing, Senator James J. Barbour described a graphic picture of the graft and corruption in Rock Island. A blackboard with a map on it and paperclips bearing cards with the names of those involved, helped jurors track movements around the downtown that fateful night.

The senator talked for seven-and-one-half hours as he outlined the conditions in Rock Island and portrayed Gabel's murder as a major incident.

*Clarence Darrow*

"The dance goes on. It's a wonderful scene next door to the vestibule of hell. And many of those who were around that night are under the ground. Snow is now falling on their graves, covering them with a mantle of purity they didn't have in life, and there are just two of the aggregation of the Rock Island News left.

"One is Myron Jordan, who says he had nothing to do with The News, and yet he reads it over to see if the articles are in his style. He has always been active in Looney's support and now is on Looney's bonds, and it is no wonder he comes here and lies in an effort to save Looney.

*Ben S. Bell*

"The other is Sinclair, and we put into evidence words out of that man's mouth, admissions he made to people who at the time he knew to be Looney's friend. Sinclair knew all about the crime, how it was to be committed, and he gets $50 a week with Looney for denying the fact," the senator charged.

"We are now at the closing of this case. We've had most of the witnesses on this stand, but there are more to be called. Think of the great inventions with which such marvelous things are accomplished these days — the telephone, the telegraph, the radio. In time, perhaps we shall go but one step further and the spirits of the dead shall come back and stand around us and pass judgment on our conduct.

*George W. Wood*

"I'll call them now from the cold, cold cemetery — the victims of the tragedy, the victims of sin. Here comes Connor. He comes with silent tread, the boy of 21. He can say nothing. Brought from the golden West, drilled in marksmanship, made to go from den of infamy to den of infamy, flashing his star, collecting filthy money for his father and, on the night of death, right there in the backyard. And later on October 6, when the rival gang swept around the corner in their cars and fired on Looney, there at this Sherman House of prostitution, receiving his petitions for the judgeship, Looney springs into the Sherman to seek protection from his man Pedigo, and Connor stands his ground, returning shot for shot until he falls dead.

*Ben Stewart*

"Riddled with bullets, this son was worthy of a better father and better life and better death.

"Eddie Miner, the manner of whose death is obscure, comes next. He who knows so much, but cannot tell us about the events that night Gabel was killed. He was shot to death in an apartment by a man that worked for the gang. Looney's gang," said Senator Barbour.

"Butch Ginnane, a devout church man he undoubtedly was, helped his chief to arm himself with a light woman. He comes here upon this witness stand. Butch Ginnane will you confess? His head falls upon his breast; his eye lights upon the bullet wound. 'Confess? I have confessed. I am a suicide. I am with the dead.'

*Charles W. Hadley*

"We must call Cleland upon this witness stand. Cleland, son of a minister, perhaps. Cleland administering justice as directed by Looney. Cleland in jail day after day. Cleland remorseful.

"And Tom Cox must come. We call Tom Cox from his grave. That chief of police must tell his story. He can't tell it now — but he told it in life. 'Helen,' he said, 'they drive out the keepers of the resorts (brothels), but you'll be the last to go.' He clung to her in life — and he clung to her in death.

"Ah, but there's still one other to be called before you," Senator Barbour went on. "Once more we must visit this cold cemetery and call forth the lifeless clay of William Gabel, and have him take the witness chair — to tell you of his bootlegging and vice and how he went to give his last final service to your country. There are the checks, mute evidence of why he is there.

"After three-and-one-half years, we have brought this man to justice and we're here before this honorable jury and this honorable judge to ask you to visit upon him his penalty — not death, but put him away behind prison bars where he can no longer harm the people of this community of Rock Island, or any other community," said Senator Barbour.

"They make their slurs about Rock Island — it is a redeemed community. It is looking toward the rising sun. It is free of its menace, its miasma and its stigma."

The senator went on, reading from Kipling's "Recessional" and concluding by saying "Lord God of hosts, be with us yet. Lest we forget, lest we forget."

Silence enveloped the room as he strode to his chair.

The trial ended abruptly when the defense announced that it would waive its closing argument. The move avoided a final closing rebuttal by Hadley with which the trial was scheduled to end. Hadley's gift of logical thought and convincing speech were well known. Looney had expressed his fear of Hadley as an opponent in the trial. The defense team used the maneuver as a means of preventing him from offering up the final impression to the jury.

But in the end it made no difference.

\* \* \* \* \*

After a month of testimony, the case went to the jury. The jury deliberated a little less than 6 hours. At 9:37 a.m. on December 23, 1925, it returned its verdict.

The jurors filed into the courtroom and into the jury box where they had spent the previous month listening to testimony. The judge asked them if they had reached a verdict. The foreman, W.E. Koffman, handed the written verdict to Circuit Court Clerk Charles W. Westerberg. He handed it to the judge, who read it silently and handed it back to the clerk.

*John Looney*

"We the jury," Westerberg read loudly, "find the defendant John P. Looney guilty of murder as charged in the indictment, and we fix his punishment at imprisonment in the penitentiary for 14 years, and we find his age to be 58 years."

John Looney sat starkly silent and outwardly unmoved when the verdict was read. His daughter, Ursula Hamblin, beside him at the trial table sat quiet for a moment but then burst into tears and wept continually until she left the courthouse with her father on his way back to jail.

After leaving the courtroom and reaching the law library adjoining it, Looney also began to cry.

The jury, it was learned, took six votes to convict him. The first vote, less than an hour after the jurors went out, found 7 for conviction, 5 for acquittal, with the second vote being the same split. The third recorded 9 and 3 and the fourth vote was 10 and 2. Finally, in the sixth vote at 10:10 p.m., the vote to convict was unanimous.

Only three votes were then needed to set the sentence. The first saw one ballot in favor of life in prison, six favoring a twenty-year term, and five favoring fourteen years. The second vote saw a swing toward the lesser fourteen-year term with eight jurors and four still voting for twenty years in prison. Finally, on the third vote they reached unanimous agreement in favor of fourteen years in prison. That vote came at 1:50 in the morning.

One juror said that the guilty verdict was fixed early, with seven jurors who were impressed by the testimony of witnesses intimately associated with Looney who told the inside story. They realized from all of the evidence that a conspiracy must have existed and that Looney, in spite of his blanket denials and alibis, must have had a motive in killing Bill Gabel.

"With the situation thoroughly grounded there, we could see no way to rid Rock Island of it unless someone was convicted," one juror said after being dismissed.

The defense made a motion for a new trial and a January hearing date was set. There would be appeals, but Looney's grip on Rock Island was finally released.

"LOONEY GUILTY OF MURDER," said headlines in The Argus.

The story lead was simple: "Guilty of murder — Fourteen years imprisonment."

The Argus editorial that day was simply titled: "NOW WE KNOW WHO KILLED BILL GABEL."

"The conviction of John P. Looney is the best Christmas present that justice could have presented to Rock Island and its neighboring cities," The Argus editorial said.

# Number 344

Letters as large as World War I headlines hit the newsstands when John Looney was convicted of murder and sentenced to a jail term of fourteen years in December 1925. Considering all of his crimes, the sentence was viewed as a light one by some citizens of Rock Island.

Looney arrived at the gate of Stateville Prison in Joliet on January 9, 1926. Construction had begun in 1916 and the prison was officially opened in March 1925. The new prison even had flush toilets, a convenience that would not be introduced at old Joliet Prison until 1956. On his arrival, Looney's trademark smirk rapidly turned to a frightened expression when he was suddenly confronted by the sight of this bleak fortress of confinement. Stateville was located six-and-a-half miles north of the old Joliet Prison on a beautifully manicured highway. Looney was lucky that he was sent to Stateville, while those found guilty of the Market Square shooting had been sent to the old Joliet Prison. Prisoners said they would rather serve a year at Stateville than six months at Joliet. As the automobile carrying Looney from Galesburg drew closer, the prison presented an imposing sight. At first the prison appeared magnificent, but as he drew closer, Looney realized what it represented and a feeling of fear gripped his body.

*John Looney*

On 64 acres of well-groomed grounds, prisoners were working on an oval-shaped garden while stone-faced guards with rifles stood stoically eyeing their every move. Looney's new home, known as "The Round House" by prisoners, was a different kind of Citadel of Sin — housing the meanest of the mean. Its inmates were some of the most desperately dangerous men on earth, confined for the commission of crimes beyond belief.

The finality of it all was something Looney had yet to fathom. Sentenced for conspiracy and murder, he was sent there to spend two to five years for conspiracy and fourteen years for murder. His prison record showed his hair color as black and gray; his age 59; his height five feet six-and-one-quarter inches; his weight 112 pounds; his residence, not mentioned; his religion, none; he stated he had an eighth-grade education and that he left home when he was 15 years old. The presiding judge who administered the sentence was Willis Graham from Monmouth, Illinois.

Looney's jail name became Number 344.

As Looney arrived, reporters met him at the gate. His voice was shaking, and he was continually coughing — coughs that shook his entire body. His face showed the scars of many fights. His nose was flattened, there were many marks on his face and he seemed beaten and torn, yet stood erect and his eyes flashed in defiance as he again declared that he would fight to prove his innocence. He told reporters that he had suffered terribly while in the Galesburg jail for his trial.

"I lost my property in the west, and all of my holdings in Rock Island," he said. He cried when asked about his son, Connor.

"He was murdered on the streets of the city — Rock Island," he said, his tears turning to anger and his agitation then directed at the "scoundrels that killed my son."

He promised reporters that his conviction would be reversed. "I have been a battler all of my life. My newspaper, the Rock Island News, battled for years and other newspapers opposed me. I've had my innings, and I suppose I'll have to take my medicine now."

Looney also claimed that his years spent out west were due to health reasons and not running from the law. "One of my lungs is affected. I didn't go out west to avoid trouble in Rock Island but rather on account of my health. I'm a bit afraid that I can't make this battle due to my health."

To pay his lawyers and finance his appeal, Looney sold his ranch in New Mexico. He had bought the land in January 1914 for $3 an acre. Needing to raise money to defray the cost of his appeal, Looney "sold" the 20,000 acres of land for $1.50 an acre. Liens and taxes he owed limited the price.

In May 1951, his daughter, Ursula Hamblin, would file a lawsuit against Edward and Estelle Sargent, attempting to reclaim the land her father had bought in 1914. The ranch had been heavily mortgaged by Samuel Thorpe on November 1, 1922, and he foreclosed on the mortgage June 20, 1925. During the time in which the Hamblins and Looney could reclaim the property from foreclosure, Mrs. Hamblin argued that she gave the deed to the ranch as security for a loan from Edward Sargent. After the option to repurchase the ranch was not executed, the Sargents were delivered a warranty deed dated February 9, 1926.

In the later court challenge, Mrs. Hamblin would argue that the land was not sold but only put up as security for a loan and the ridiculously low price should be proof of that. Sargent claimed that he bought Horse Lake Ranch.

On July 1, 1952, the jury rejected Mrs. Hamblin's claim and ordered her to pay the Sargents' court costs. The Hamblins were living in Luna City, New Mexico, at the time. A ranch hand for the Sargents said that when it was taken over, Looney's ranch was not much more than some ramshackle buildings — not very impressive by any standards. Auto bodies were found in Horse Lake, he said.

* * * * *

While Stateville was considered better than Joliet, it was no picnic. In 1928, a special panel, the Clabough Commission, was formed to study conditions at the prison. It found that being a guard at the prison wasn't much better than being a convict. It noted that 225 guards watched 3,400 inmates, and "most of the guards are called hayseeds by the convicts." Every constraint on the prisoner was also a constraint on the guards. They had no tenure, no pension, they were ill paid and untrained. They often had to work sixteen-hour days and there were only enough beds to accommodate half of the men. Guards could have no conversation with the inmates.

The report found that discipline was arbitrary and capricious. Lockup in solitary confinement was accompanied by "stringing up" — requiring the inmates to stand handcuffed to the bars eight hours a day for as long as 15 days. During the ordeal, the prisoner was given one slice of bread and one glass of water per day.

The staff was so small that the inmates did much of the work at the prison. This gave convicts terrific privileges, particularly those who formed the power hierarchy inside. Between 1925 and 1932, Stateville was marked by violence among the inmates and members of the staff. The absence of a capable administration made this period lawless and violent. Gang leaders set up shacks in the yard and sold young offenders as homosexual prostitutes. Gambling flourished throughout the prison. In 1926, the year Looney arrived, seven inmates took the deputy warden hostage and stabbed him to death when he refused at knife point to cooperate in their escape. In 1931, a large riot at Stateville resulted in more than a half million dollars in damages from the rampage and burning. One prisoner was killed, and the entire prison was on lockdown for seven months.

Upon Looney's arrival at prison, the inspecting physician reported that he was suffering from a lung infection, but had not determined it to be tuberculosis. He said Looney was very run down, very depressed both physically and mentally.

Jail reports said that Looney was assigned to a cell in one of the circular cell houses at the new prison. He had no cell mate because his constant coughing and complaining annoyed the other prisoners. Fearing the dissension his presence created, Dr. Frank J. Chmelik, the prison physician, ordered Looney confined to the hospital as much as possible. Otherwise, his idle hours were spent reading books borrowed from the prison library. Prison records showed him to be a good prisoner with no infractions or discipline on his record.

Despite their dislike for him, other prisoners often sought him out for "prison lawyer" advice when making appeals to the parole board. Using his background as a lawyer, Looney drafted many well-reasoned pleas and was successful in securing reduced sentences for others, though he was never able to win his own freedom.

Officials also noted that his frailty prevented them from assigning him any heavy labor duties in the prison shops. When able to work, he was a water carrier and messenger in the yards, where construction of new buildings was going on.

Seven months into his prison stay, Dr. W.R. Fletcher reported that Looney was in fair health. The hospital had failed to find a tubercular infection despite exhaustive testing. For years, Looney's persistent bronchial infection continued to be undiagnosed. It was not until years later that it would be decided that he suffered from a lung fungus caused by dust from chicken coops or from other birds such as pigeons.

Looney spent weeks in the hospital or confined to a cot in his cell for treatment. Early on he showed constant depression and was very despondent, but perked up whenever it became possible that he might be paroled. In 1928, he was unable to do any prison work, other than to occasionally perform light tasks such as cleaning the corridors. He was able to walk from his cell to the dining hall and to attend chapel service.

Dining halls at Stateville were huge circular rooms with a rotunda in the center where the captain in charge stood. Tables made of terrazzo extended out from the center. Each pair of tables was served by a steam table with aluminum plates stacked at one end. Inmates would fill their plates cafeteria-style, which helped keep the food hot. Waiters would then walk between tables with bread and coffee and second helpings were served from a large portable pot, which a waiter wore strapped to him. Prisoners could have as many helpings as they wanted.

*John Looney's prison photo*

At the tap of the captain's cane, the waiters withdrew from the aisles. At two taps in succession, the men at the first table rose and filed out, followed in turn by the next row and then the next. Inmates proceeded up the metal stairs and around the gallery to their cells. The doors of all cells in the four floors of "The Round House" faced the central guard tower. The doors were pulled shut and a few minutes later a bell would ring and prisoners would have to stand at the door until the two jailers completed counting the prisoners.

Immediately upon his conviction, Looney's daughter, Ursula, started a strenuous fight to overturn the conviction and then to have him freed early. His conviction was upheld in February 1927. Several times she filed with the Board of Pardons to have her father released for poor health.

The first application for a pardon was rejected in September 1931. It was the contention of his daughter that he would die in prison if not released. He had spent much of his time in the prison hospital, and his work had been curtailed. When he was out of the hospital, he worked at times feeding the chickens, doing light work on the farm or working in the library.

In 1933, Mrs. Hamblin asked for parole again. In September of that year, it was reported that Looney had suffered a hemorrhage in the prison hospital, but news the next day was that he had rallied during the night and seemed to be in an improved condition. Mrs. Hamblin had been called to her father's bedside, according to news reports.

Governor Henry Horner asked Dr. Frank J. Jirka, state health director, to make an examination of Looney as part of the pardon process. The pardon request also spurred a protest from Rock Island County States Attorney Francis C. King. At the time, Looney was reportedly seriously ill in the prison hospital. But no evidence was found by Dr. Jirka that Looney was near death, and that request was also denied.

Then in March of 1934, Warden Frank D. Whipp announced that Looney would become eligible for early discharge on April 8, after having served eight years and three months of his fourteen-year sentence. Looney was in the prison hospital at the time.

At 5:10 a.m. on April 7, 1934, the former Rock Island vice lord was released from Stateville Prison.

* * * * *

Looney's life as the son of immigrants had started poor, but full. While the rest of his family in Ottawa worked hard to pull themselves up by the bootstraps, John Looney had always looked for shortcuts. His hero in life was Robert Emmet, an Irish patriot who urged revolt and broke the law in an effort to rid his country of what he perceived to be English oppression. Looney tried to justify his own lawlessness in much the same way. Like Emmet, he was small in stature and lean on social status. His world was one of fantasies. His psyche was that of a psychopath, respected only by other criminals and feared by everyone else.

Finally, his confinement and punishment was over. Once again, John Looney had cut corners and been released early.

The sun was peeking through a low fog when Looney left the prison where he had been confined since 1926. He shuffled out of jail withered and broken — in mind and body. At age 68, there would be no starting over. A life marked by excesses and violence was now on the downhill side. He was without friends and penniless, except for the $10 given him when he left prison. Racked by health problems, he was just a frail shell of his former self as he tottered feebly through the gates of the prison at sunrise.

Looney greeted his daughter as she met him at the reception building located at the outer gates of the prison. Ursula kissed him on the left cheek and assisted him to her waiting automobile.

Looney was asked if he had anything to say by two sleepy-eyed reporters who had waited since early in the morning.

"No," he whispered, his voice weak from his ongoing bronchial disease.

Mrs. Hamblin was equally evasive. She refused to say where she was taking him, although prison officials said it was to her home in Warsaw, Texas. While most prisoners at the time were released around 8 or 9 in the morning, Looney was released earlier at the request of his daughter, who said she wanted to drive him as far as possible that day. He was officially checked out the day before to save as much time as possible, although his reduced sentence officially ended at midnight.

Before leaving prison, Looney was outfitted in a tan suit, gray hat and overcoat, shirt, underclothing, socks and shoes, and was given $10 — the sum given to all departing prisoners.

Ursula Hamblin also had little to say when contacted the night before at the hotel she had been staying at for several days awaiting her father's release.

"My father is innocent. I never tried to have him paroled. But I did try to have him released because he is not guilty. There is a lot to say on our side, but it's too late now to say it."

She refused to answer all other questions.

Frail and fatigued from the excitement of his release, John Looney was helped by his daughter as he walked to her car. In his pocket he carried a bottle of cough medicine. He coughed several times as he was being placed in the back seat of the auto, which had been stuffed with pillows and blankets to make him more comfortable.

In a low voice, Looney objected to something his daughter had done or said.

"Shush, don't say anything. The reporters may hear," she told him.

Looney then settled into his seat as the car drove off. A brief stop was made at the honor farm to retrieve a watch, several rings and some money Looney had on deposit there. The car's wheels kicked up dust as the two began their long journey to Texas.

He never returned to Rock Island.

# No markers for the graves

It wasn't a pretty picture when John Looney met his daughter at the same gate he'd entered. A couple of reporters waited, but Looney could barely speak as he coughed and gasped for air.

Ursula Hamblin vowed she would never return to the community that had sent her father to prison. "Rock Island is dead to me," she had said.

While the plan had been to leave immediately for Texas, they apparently went first to the family's home in Ottawa to visit relatives and friends. They then proceeded on to Texas, where Ursula lived with her husband, Frank, and daughter. Frank was a ranch handler and experienced oil-field worker. It was a nomadic existence at best, constantly moving from place to place, rarely staying long anywhere.

Ursula fretted over her father's health to the dismay of her husband. It likely affected their marriage. While Frank worked in west Texas, John Looney was placed in a sanitarium in El Paso for some time, but his discomfort at that institute soon had Ursula moving him to Roswell, New Mexico, where they owned a small home.

She kept Looney with the family when they moved again to south Texas. Ranch work was scarce and more and more oil fields were springing up around the state. While in an oil field camp near McAllen, Looney's health deteriorated and he became difficult to care for. It was a miserable situation for all of the family. Looney took a turn for the worse. His last weeks and days were wrenching — a slow, painful ending to his tumultuous life.

Looney struggled with an illness that could not be cured. His last reflections were of his boyhood home in Ottawa: the memory of his father traveling that old road from the depot to town; the wonderful Sunday gatherings and laughter of his sisters and brothers. There were memories of his father's dramatic description of Emmet's death in Ireland, beautiful Ireland; the flowers at his unexpected wedding to Nora; and, Connor, his poor boy Connor, murdered on the streets of Rock Island.

"By persistence some man may, at last, take my life," Looney once wrote, "but never a man can take my death — that sweet which medicines all pain."

He never forgot his father's words, Emmet's words: "No markers on the graves of our family until Ireland is finally free." The smirk came back again, if just for the last time. "I will never give up," he thought, but it was over. Looney was home at

## RECORD OF DEATHS

791 — MANUFACTURED BY STAFFORD-LOWDON CO. FORT WORTH — 99575

**TEXAS DEPARTMENT OF HEALTH**
**BUREAU OF VITAL STATISTICS**
STANDARD CERTIFICATE OF DEATH

1. PLACE OF DEATH STATE OF TEXAS COUNTY OF *Brooks*

CITY OR PRECINCT NO. *# R.F.D. Falfurrias    15 mi. W. Rachele, Prect. #4*
GIVE STREET AND NUMBER OR NAME OF INSTITUTION

2. FULL NAME OF DECEASED *John P. Looney*

LENGTH OF RESIDENCE WHERE DEATH OCCURRED _____ YEARS *6* MONTHS _____ DAYS (SOCIAL SECURITY NO.)

RESIDENCE OF THE DECEASED, STREET AND NO. CITY *Alta Mesa* COUNTY *Brooks* STATE *Texas*

PERSONAL AND STATISTICAL PARTICULARS

3. SEX *Male*
4. COLOR OR RACE *White*
5. SINGLE, MARRIED, WIDOWED OR DIVORCED (WRITE THE WORD) *Widowed*
6. DATE OF BIRTH *Nov. 5, 1866*
7. AGE *75* YEARS *4* MONTHS *7* DAYS IF LESS THAN 1 DAY HOURS / MIN.
8A. TRADE, PROFESSION OR KIND OF WORK DONE *Ret. Rancher*
8B. INDUSTRY OR BUSINESS IN WHICH ENGAGED
9. BIRTHPLACE (STATE OR COUNTRY) *Illinois*
10. NAME *Patrick Looney*
11. BIRTHPLACE (STATE OR COUNTRY) *Ireland*
12. MAIDEN NAME *Margaret Maloney*
13. BIRTHPLACE (STATE OR COUNTRY) *Ireland*
14. SIGNATURE
ADDRESS *Box 247 Falfurrias, TEXAS*
15. PLACE OF BURIAL OR REMOVAL *McAllen, TEXAS*
DATE *3/14 — 1942*
16. SIGNATURE *Kreidler, Funeral Home*
ADDRESS *McAllen, TEXAS*

MEDICAL PARTICULARS

17. DATE OF DEATH *Mar. 12, 1942*
18. I HEREBY CERTIFY THAT I ATTENDED THE DECEASED FROM *Mar 7, 1942* TO *Mar 12, 1942*
I LAST SAW H. ALIVE ON *Mar 11, 1942*
THE DEATH OCCURRED ON THE DATE STATED ABOVE AT _____ M.
THE PRIMARY CAUSE OF DEATH WAS: *Fungus infection of lung*    DURATION
CONTRIBUTORY CAUSES WERE: *senility*

IF NOT DUE TO DISEASE, SPECIFY WHETHER:
ACCIDENT, SUICIDE, OR HOMICIDE
DATE OF OCCURRENCE
PLACE OF OCCURRENCE
MANNER OR MEANS
IF RELATED TO OCCUPATION OF DECEASED, SPECIFY
SIGNATURE *W. H. Duncan* M. D.
ADDRESS *McAllen, TEXAS* COR.

20. FILE NUMBER *558*    FILE DATE *Mar. 13, 1942*    SIGNATURE OF LOCAL REGISTRAR *J. J. Benavides*    POSTOFFICE ADDRESS *Falfurrias, TEXAS*

IF DECEASED HAS RENDERED MILITARY SERVICE, FILL OUT THE FOLLOWING:
(1) IS THE DECEASED REPORTED TO HAVE BEEN IN SUCH SERVICE?    (2) NAME OF ORGANIZATION IN WHICH SERVICE WAS RENDERED?    (3) SERIAL NUMBER OF DISCHARGE PAPERS OR ADJUSTED SERVICE CERTIFICATE?
(4) NAME OF NEXT OF KIN OR OF NEXT FRIEND?    POST OFFICE ADDRESS?

IF DECEASED IS UNKNOWN NON-RESIDENT, FILL OUT THE FOLLOWING:
(A) COLOR OF HAIR?    (B) COLOR OF EYES?    (C) HEIGHT?    FEET    INCHES
(D) WEIGHT?    (E) DEFORMITIES?    (F) TATTOO MARKS?
(G) OTHER MARKS OF IDENTIFICATION?

last. He no longer felt pain and torment. This ending was the only real peace he ever had.

"They will never forget me, like me or hate me," John Looney was quoted as once saying. He also said, "Those who contend against me are not my enemies. They are my friends because through them my name is becoming immortalized." Even today, from that long-ago era, there is still a lingering feeling in Rock Island about John Looney. He will never be forgiven; nor will he be forgotten.

John Looney was the forerunner to the gangsters of Prohibition, the '20s and the '30s. He was a crime boss long before Al Capone and others made it fashionable and glamorous. He devised an organized system, dividing his business into separate units, and used his newspaper as a "hammer" over his enemies and detractors. Eventually, Chicago, Detroit, New York and other large metropolitan areas adopted his "organized" crime technique.

The G-Men said that Looney had the largest and best-organized criminal business they had ever seen.

For years after Looney's fall, court records in the Tri-Cities showed more arrests for illegal gambling, rampant liquor sales, prostitution, fines for illegal saloon operations, barrel-of-fun tickets, punch-board operations, and card games with high stakes. But there was no John Looney, no organized crime boss. Today, Rock Island proudly embraces its historic past, but not the lawlessness that was a part of that era.

Removed from under the shadow of John Looney, many of the other players from this period in history went on to live productive lives in the community.

Jennie Mills, a prominent madam in Rock Island, was well known throughout the nation for her parlors and the numerous girls she provided for her clients. Despite her notorious business, she also made many charitable contributions during her life. She conducted business from 308 22nd Street in Rock Island, including the Eat Shop (which didn't serve food) up until her death, February 6, 1958, at age 87.

Anthony Billburg moved from Centerville, Iowa, to Davenport in 1905, marrying Margaret Alexander the same year. Billburg owned several saloons, including one known for the longest bar in the world, employed prostitutes with his wife as the madam, hosted high-stakes gambling and is remembered by history as a key enemy of Looney. His wife died in January 1935. Tony Billburg died at his home, 221½ 20th Street, Rock Island, on July 31, 1950, after suffering for years from emphysema.

*Anthony Billburg in his later years, just prior to his death.*

George Holsapple, born in LeClaire, Iowa, was the son of Captain William Holsapple, a well-known river-boat captain. He married Mamie Thomson in 1906 in Davenport. After serving his jail term for the murder of Connor Looney, he returned to Rock Island, where he died July 20, 1966, at age 87.

Wallace William (W.W.) Wilmerton was one of three children born in Preemption to William Wilmerton, a cousin of author James Fennimore Cooper. He was born November 7, 1861, and was a prominent farmer for many years until moving to Rock Island and becoming a newspaper publisher, leading to his feud and shootout with Looney. Wilmerton died January 31, 1936, at Moline City

Hospital, at age 74. He was survived by his wife, Anna, a daughter, three sons, four grandchildren and one great-grandchild.

William Scott was indicted during the Looney era as a co-conspirator in extorting money from prostitution and gambling. He was never convicted and restarted his career as an attorney, practicing law for more than 50 years in Rock Island. He was Rock Island city attorney from 1899 to 1904, when he was elected States Attorney for Rock Island County. He and his wife, Amy, lived in a special Queen Anne-style home at 1038 21st Street in Rock Island, which is on the National Register of Historic Places. He also served as U.S. Consulate in Switzerland. The Scotts lived in this home from 1904 to 1948, when they moved to Apartment 4, 2644 Harrison Street in Davenport. His brother was Judge William Scott of Davenport. After his wife's death in 1956, William Scott lived with his cousin, Marguerite Brooks, at 1204 Iowa Street, Davenport, until his death, September 11, 1963.

*Jacob Ramser*

Harry Schriver, the son of Captain W.H. Schriver of rural Edgington Township, was an attorney who was first elected Rock Island mayor in 1911, serving until 1915. He was elected again in 1919 and served until 1923. He attended Reynolds Village High School and graduated from Valparaiso University in northern Indiana. He never married. When he died November 7, 1959, at age 87, there was no mention of his conspiracy conviction or the turbulent Looney era in his life. The photo accompanying his obituary showed a white-haired man with thick-rimmed glasses and a thin face, with a slight, kindly smile.

*Minnie Potter*

Jacob Ramser continued to operate his optometrist and jeweler business at 209 18th Street, Rock Island, until his death, October 30, 1934. Ramser died suddenly at home of a heart ailment. He left his wife, daughter, Virginia, and son, Eugene, at home, and another son, Jacob Ramser III.

By the dawn of the 20th century, John W. Potter established the Rock Island Argus as a major news source. He died in 1898 following surgery. His widow, the former Minnie Estelle Abbott, carried on his vision. It was Minnie Potter's courage and determination that kept The Argus alive during a critical 25-year battle with Looney's Rock Island News. Her sons joined the business in 1920. Mrs. Potter died from the second of two heart attacks on June 6, 1936, and her death resulted in consolidation of power with her three children. The newspaper continued in operation by the family until 1986, when it was sold to the Small Newspaper Group.

Lawrence Pedigo, a leading crime figure during the days of Looney, went on to become an aviation pioneer in the Tri-Cities region. He was instrumental in developing Cram Field airport in Davenport, where he became the general manager. He held a government transport pilot's license and was a member of the National Aeronautic Association and also conducted the Mississippi Valley Flying School. He died January 24, 1933, at age 37.

Louis Ortell, Looney's collector, confidant, a tavern owner, gambler, extorter and general workhorse for the Looney crime organization, was a resident of Rock Island for 50 years. He was born August 10, 1878, in Red Bank, New Jersey, and moved to Moline as a small boy and attended school there. Ortell was involved in virtually every illegal activity Looney attempted and was indicted several times but never convicted. He was granted immunity to testify at the Looney trial and then returned to Rock Island as if nothing had happened. He ran a variety of businesses including his tavern and pool hall at 1505-1507 2nd Avenue in Rock Island. He managed a service station, a second-hand goods store, and sold real estate until his death, October 9, 1946.

Myron Jordan worked at Looney's newspaper for many years and wrote many antagonistic and libelous stories about citizens of Rock Island. He was born in 1869 in nearby Orion, Illinois, where he learned the printing trade. Jordan was one of the few who remained loyal to Looney to the end, even testifying in his defense at his trial in Galesburg. He was a complicated man with ideals that many found disturbing, however, he was considered knowledgeable when it came to printing. He died suddenly June 24, 1938, at the United States Veterans Hospital at Hines, Illinois, from an attack of pneumonia that followed an operation on his sinuses.

Frank Kelly, Looney's original law partner, died October 16, 1911, after he tripped and fell under the wheels of a street car in front of the home of his father, Patrick H. Kelly, at 2034 Fifth Avenue. Both of his legs were amputated, but the shock caused his death within very few minutes.

Thomas Cox had served as a patrolman with the Rock Island police department beginning in 1907 and served as chief from 1919 to December 1922. He was named chief under the second administration of Harry Schriver. He was indicted, but died October 13, 1924, before facing trial. He had been in failing health for 18 months before his death.

*Thomas Cox*

Dan Drost was a native of Rock Island, born April 12, 1860. After being sentenced to prison for the murder of Connor Looney, he returned to Rock Island where he hung around the Harper and Harms Hotels and lived downtown. The Looney era had been a horrifying time that he just wanted to forget. People didn't really know him or care about him at the end. He died in October 1939, at age 79.

*Dan Drost*

For years, Emeal Davis worked on the railroad pounding nails into the tracks of the Rock Island Line. He saved his money and bought a saloon in Davenport called the Red Rose Saloon, a "black and tan joint" located on the edge of Bucktown. If Looney needed a problem dealt with, Emeal was his man after Looney's falling out with Billburg. Davis' specialty was transporting girls and booze for Looney. He also delivered stolen cars. Davis appeared to be mild-mannered, but he had a hard side. He was pressured to testify against Looney at the Gabel murder trial, but his testimony was sometimes beneficial to Looney. After the trial, he left Rock Island and was later seen working for the railroad in LaSalle-Peru, but it is unknown what happened to him after that.

Helen Van Dale grew from an innocent girl who turned her first "trick" at age 16, to the chief executive of a nationwide prostitution network, becoming an icon in the field. Beautiful, proud and haughty, she thought herself invincible until passage of the Mann White Slave Act.

All Mrs. Van Dale was worried about was keeping her girls busy, but the crime organization crumbled around them. Her suitor, Chief Cox, got unnerved and in over his head. He became more violent and started to panic. Meanwhile, The Argus kept turning up the heat.

Mrs. Van Dale was caught transporting girls from Rock Island to Davenport, something she had done many times before. The charge was interstate transportation of girls for immoral purposes. While she was awaiting trial, a deal was cut to drop the charges in exchange for her giving up the business and testifying against John Looney for the murder of Bill Gabel. She didn't like Looney much, and didn't mind giving him up, but refused to testify against the others. She was the chief witness against Looney in the trial held in her old home town. After his trial, charges against her were dropped. She was only 32 years old, but aged beyond her years.

After three earlier marriages, and her affair with Cox, Helen met Eddie Wriedt, a Davenport salesman who visited one of her establishments, and they drank up a storm. She worked her charms on Eddie, as she had so many others, and soon he became her fourth husband. But April 25, 1925, eight months before Looney's conviction, he died of pneumonia. Helen bought several lots from Eddie's father and buried him in Fairmount Cemetery in Davenport's west end.

After Looney's trial, Helen's sister "Dimples" and her mother stayed in an apartment in downtown Davenport for a time, and then moved to LaSalle, Illinois, to put their past behind them. They returned to Davenport to rescue Helen before the booze killed her. She moved in with them until she recovered. It was there that Helen would meet "the love of her life," Irvin Joseph Wonders, a laborer who owned a sandwich shop. On March 28, 1929, he became husband number five for Helen, but he would be her last. He was 27. She was 35.

They made their home in Peru, but Helen missed her old haunts and convinced her new husband that they could turn the old Palmer Inn in Nahant into a reputable restaurant and hotel and make money in the process. They bought the place with her mother's money and began renovating the building. On September 30, 1941, her mother sold the building to Helen for one dollar. On November 4, 1943, Irvin and his

*The Palmer Inn in Nahant wasn't much, but offered a new start for Helen Van Dale. Her mother bought the inn and sold it to Van Dale in 1941. But when her husband was killed getting supplies to renovate the building, she was devastated and left the area for good.*

friend, Frank Majchtzak, were working on the building and drove into town for supplies. They were driving south, crossing the railroad tracks by the roundhouse, when a Rock Island Lines train running east and traveling about 35 mile per hour struck the car broadside at the Harbor Road crossing and dragged it about two blocks. Both men were crushed to death. Helen, devastated by the death of her husband, left the area. Despondent, she moved back with her mother.

Irvin Wonders was buried near Eddie Wriedt in Fairmount Cemetery.

Helen wanted a new life and fresh identity. She changed her name and lived out her years as Eula H. Wonders, a name she apparently borrowed from Eulogia — from her early passion for Greek history. She died in a hospital in LaSalle on December 13, 1951, at age 58, and was buried between Eddie and Irvin. A tragic ending to a whirlwind life? Only Helen could answer that. Her mother, Nancy, 82, died the next summer on August 22, 1952, and was buried next to her daughter.

Eddie and Irvin have headstones. Like the Looney family, Helen and her mother do not.

Ursula Hamblin would live her life out in New Mexico and Texas, dying in Austin in February 1984, at age 87. Her final resting place has not been found, but is likely an unmarked grave somewhere in Austin or perhaps San Antonio, where she lived for a while with relatives. Frank Hamblin preceded her in death in August 1969, at age 74, at Ingleside on the Bay, San Patricio, Texas, near Corpus Christi. Their daughter, Kathaleene, later married and had at least two children. If she is alive today, she would be in her eighties and her children in their late fifties.

No records have been found on Ursula's sister, Kathleen (Sister Mary), who became a nun and lived her adult life in St. Louis, Missouri.

After John Looney's death, a simple funeral took place.

One newspaper obituary read: "Funeral services for John P. Looney, 75, who died at the home of his daughter, Mrs. Frank Hamblin, at the Standard Oil camp west of Falfurrias, Texas, Thursday night, were held at Our Lady of Sorrows Church Saturday morning with Father John officiating. Interment was in Roselawn Cemetery, McAllen, Texas, under the direction of the Kreidler Funeral home. Mr. Looney was a retired rancher and was a native of Illinois. He is survived by his two daughters, Mrs. Hamblin and Sister Mary of Placid at the Good Shepherd Convent of St. Louis, Missouri. Pallbearers were B.B. Brown, P.T. Kerner, E.B. Frazer, H.C. Chaney, David Bellard and Walter Pilgrim, McAllen, Texas."

The manager at Roselawn Cemetery said that Looney's was a strange and lonely grave. The site was hard to locate and was found in a remote section in the far end of the cemetery, by a fence. There was nothing there to remember him by, only a card in the file and an "x" on the cemetery map. Our inquiry was the first since she had worked there.

The grave is only covered by high, waving grass.

There is no headstone.

**JOHN P. LOONEY**

FALFURRIAS—John P. Looney, 75, who made his home with his daughter, Mrs. Frank L. Hamlin, at the Standard Oil camp west of here died this week.

A retired rancher, Looney was a native of Illinois.

He is survived by the daughter with whom he made his home and another daughter, Sister Mary of St. Placid at the Good Shepherd convent, St. Louis, Mo.

Funeral services were held at Our Lady of Sorrows Catholic church, McAllen, and interment was at Rose Lawn cemetery there under the direction of the Kreidler Funeral home.

Pallbearers were B. B. Brown, P. T. Keener, E. B. Frasier, H. C. Chaney, David Belle, and Walter Pilgrim.

# Sources

## Newspapers

We would like to thank the editors and reporters of these newspapers for their detailed and accurate coverage: The Rock Island Argus, The Rock Island Union, The Rock Island News, The Ottawa Free Press, Ottawa Free Trader, The Ottawa Journal, The Ottawa Fair Dealer, The Ottawa Daily Times, Davenport Daily Times, Davenport Times-Democrat, Milan Independent, McAllen Monitor, Davenport Democrat and Leader, Northeastern Reporter, Moline Dispatch, The Santa Fe New Mexican, The Nora Cooperative News, Tri City Journal, Chicago Record Herald, The Orion Gazette, Kansas City Star, Fort Madison Daily Democrat, Iowa City Press Citizen, Marshalltown Times-Republican, Keokuk Daily Gate City, The Burlington Hawk Eye, Clinton Herald, Colfax Tribune, The Des Moines Register, Dubuque Telegraph Herald, Cambridge Chronicle, Joliet Herald-News, Bureau County Republican, Quincy Herald Whig, Springfield State Journal Register, The Sterling Gazette, LaSalle News-Tribune, Monmouth Daily Journal, Paris Beacon-News, Peoria Journal Star, Chicago Tribune, Galesburg Register-Mail, Kewanee Star-Courier.

## Libraries

We would like to thank the staff of the following libraries for their assistance in research for this book: Bettendorf (Iowa) Public Library; Wheaton (Ill.) Historical Building; Santa Fe, (N.M.) Public Library; Knox College Special Collections Library, Galesburg, Ill.; Rock Island (Ill.) County Law Library; Rock Island County Clerk's Office; Supreme Court of Illinois Library; Newberry Library Special Collections, Chicago; Reddick Library, Ottawa; Third District Appellate Court Library, Ottawa; Moline (Ill.) Public Library; Clinton (Iowa) Public Library; Davenport (Iowa) Public Library; Richardson-Sloane Special Collections Center; Peru (Ill.) Public Library; Rock Island Public Library; Illinois State Library; Illinois State Archives; Illinois Reference Bureau; Paris (Ill.) Carnegie Public Library; Library of Peoria (Ill.) Historical Society at Bradley University, Peoria, Ill.; Peoria Public Library; Brookens Library Regional Archives Depository, University of Illinois, Springfield; Augustana College Public Library Archives, Rock Island; Fort Madison (Iowa) Public Library; Burlington (Iowa) Public Library; Joliet (Ill.)

Public Library; El Paso (Texas) Public Library; Ottawa (Ill.) Public Library; Monmouth (Ill.) Public Library; Galesburg (Ill.) Public Library; Knoxville (Ill.) Public Library; LaSalle- Peru (Ill.) Public Library; Albuquerque (N. Mex.) Library.

## Publications

Some facts and insight into the period were provided by the following publications: "Inside the World's Toughest Prison," "The Rock Island Railroad Digest," "Then Was the Good Old Days" by W.L Purcell, "Hell at Midnight in Davenport, or The History of the City's Shame" by William Lloyd Clark, "Rock Island — Down the Great River" by Capt. William Glazier, "The Railroadians of America — Album of Railroad Stations," "Depots in Illinois," "Voices of Kerry" by Jimmy Wolfe, "Discovering Kerry" by T.J. Barrington, "Man Against The Mob" by William Roehmer, "The Horseman's Encyclopedia" by Margaret Cabell Self, "Robert Emmet" by Ruan O'Donnell, "Radical Irish Lives" by Ruan O'Donnell, "Tread Softly on My Dreams" by Gretta Curran Browne, "Journal of Illinois History," "American Bar Assn. Journal," "Gale Directory," bucktownsaga.com.

## Official Sources

"Citadel of Sin" includes information from the following official sources: U.S. Census; Social Security records; Brooks County (Texas) Court House, Falfurrias, Texas; State of Texas Research; Corpus Christi News & Historical Center; El Paso (Texas) Historical Society; McAllen, Texas, Historical Society; Kreidler Funeral Parlor, McAllen, Texas; LaSalle County (Ill.) Genealogy Guild; Hildago County, McAllen, Texas; FBI Headquarters, History Dept., Washington, D.C.; Rio Grande Historical Collection, New Mexico State University, Las Cruces, N.M.; New Mexico Records Center & Archives; Rock Island Preservation Society, Rock Island, Ill.; Warren County Historical Society, Monmouth, Ill.; Edgard County Genealogical Library, Paris, Ill.; Edgard County Historical Society, Paris, Ill.; Peoria Historical Society, Peoria, Ill.; Galesburg Historical Society, Galesburg, Ill.; Knox County Genealogical Society, Galesburg, Ill.; Joliet Historical Society and Museum, Joliet Ill.; Knoxville County Museum, Knoxville, Ill.; Rock Island County Historical Society, Rock Island, Ill.; Warren County Genealogical Society, Monmouth, Ill.; Calumet City Historical Society Museum, Calumet City, Ill.; Chicago Genealogical Society, Chicago, Ill.; Chicago Historical Society, Chicago, Ill.; Chicago-Edgewater Historical Society, Chicago, Ill.; Hyde Park Historical Society, Chicago, Ill.; Irish American Heritage Center, Chicago, Ill.; Elmhurst Historical Museum, Elmhurst, Ill.; LeClaire (Iowa) Museum and Cemetery Records; Rio Arriba County History, Chama, New Mexico.

# Individuals

We would especially like to thank these individuals for their special contributions to this effort: Helen Crawford and other Looney family members, Ottawa, Ill.; Bill Maloney, Parish Clerk, St. Columba Church & Cemetery; Judy Klinger, Santa Fe Public Library; Marta Estrada, Border Heritage Center, El Paso Public Library; Lewis B. Wilson; Mrs. Helen Forsberg; Marguerite Reidy; Eleanore Beauchamp Peterson; Fred Heffernan; Lewis Cochran; Karen Kitchen; Judge Steven Mathers; Suzanne Curry; Uncle "Will" Van Fossen; Alice Dailing; Tom Cutter; Judge Dave DeDonker; Joe Kelly Jr.; Jim Arpy; Joe Senatra; Judge John Bell's Journals; Greg Vogele, Chippiannock Cemetery Heritage Foundation, Rock Island, Ill.; William Graham.

# Special Acknowledgments

- Suzanne Curry (dec) for her efforts and suggestions
- Judy Belan, formerly of Augustana College Library Special Collections, Rock Island, Ill. You name it, she found it.
- Mrs. Helen Crawford and relatives of the Looney clan in Ottawa for sharing their family's history
- John Whiteside (dec), The Herald-New, Joliet, for his help and historical insight
- "Uncle Will" Van Fossen (dec.) He lived it on Old Harbor Road in Nahant, Iowa.
- Fred Heffernan, relative of Louie Ortell and the Frank Kelly family.
- Joe Senatra, expert on early Rock Island.
- Alice Dailing, who helped compile original notes into type-written sequence.
- Tom Cutter (dec.) grandson of Anthony Billburg, for his insight into the family and Clarence Darrow.
- Judge Dave DeDonker, Looney historian for his views on the Looney trials.
- Joe Kelly Jr. on his father Judge J.P. Kelly and the Kelly era.
- Sally Hutchcraft, Knoxville Historical Society and historian on St. Mary's School For Girls, Knoxville.